MILFORD NECK

A SHORT HISTORY

COMPILED AND WRITTEN

By L. ROLAND BEEBE

Dover Litho Printing
1211 N. Dupont Hwy
Dover, DE 19901

THOMPSON STORE & HOUSE

EARLY CAR WASH IN MILFORD NECK
Courtesy of Mrs. Sarah Webb

THIS BOOK IS DEDICATED TO THE
MEMORY OF MY FATHER AND DAUGHTER
LAWRENCE BEEBE & SUSAN DIANE BEEBE

This, the first edition on this book,
has been limited to five hundred copies.

THIS IS BOOK NO. ....

Please direct all correspondence and book orders to:

LRB ENTERPRISES
P.O. BOX 449
MILFORD, DE 19963

CONTENTS

LIST OF ILLUSTRATIONS

BEER'S MAP OF 1868

Courtesy of Delaware State Archives

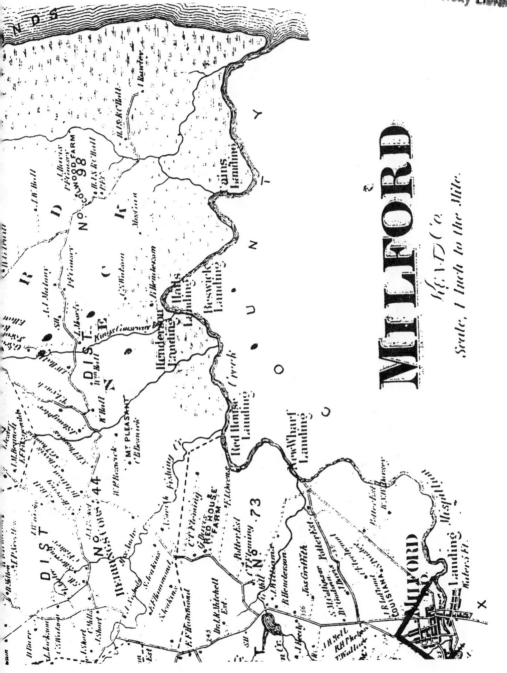

MILFORD

KENT Co.

Scale, 1 Inch to the Mile.

INTRODUCTION

It has been said that when Mr. Harvey Thompson's house was sold the auctioneer, Burt Willis, remarked "You might find a better house, but you will never find a better community." Since living here for the past nineteen years I can attest to that fact. I purchased Mr. Harvey's property in July, 1971. After owning the property and talking with friends and neighbors I started to learn a lot about the Thompson Store, now in Lewes, and the history of the Sardis Church. In discussing the history of the area I became interested in the age and history of my house. I decided to research the owners of my property to see how far I could trace its history. That is how this book came about, the further my research took me the more I learned about Milford Neck. I felt a need to share the information I obtained with the people of the area. It also became apparent, while looking for information, that no one has ever compiled a history of Milford Neck, in one volume, up to this point.

Several institutions and many individuals made the production of this volume possible. I am greatly indebted to the staff of the Delaware State Archives for their assistance and cooperation. I also wish to thank the offices of the Kent County deeds and wills, the Sussex County deeds and wills, the Delaware State Library in Dover and the Barrett's Chapel Museum. All of these provided endless sources of information and were very helpful in guiding me to my goal.

I would like to thank all who furnished me with pictures and allowed me to published them. They will be acknowledged below each picture throughout the book.

I am forever grateful to my enthusiastic and helpful guides for providing me with interviews, sources of information and continued support until this project was completed.

EARLY WRITINGS

I am starting this section with a sketch of Isaac R. Jester, who's writings you will soon be enjoying. Mr. Jester, between May 1907 and April 1909, intermittently had a series of articles published in the Milford Chronicle.

I would like to take this opportunity to thank the Chronicle for allowing me to include them in this book. As you read these articles try to picture the people and the area as it was at the time of their writing.

I hope as you read through the latter part of this book that my research will bring about a clearer picture of the history of this area of Delaware.

ISAAC R. JESTER

EDUCATOR - HISTORIAN

1836 - 1912

Isaac R. Jester was one of the most widely known citizens of Kent County. Mr. Jester was born, the second child of a family of eleven, August 4, 1836 to John Taylor Jester and Mary Richard Jester.

He had very little educational advantages, but by continued application he acquired a through knowledge of the elementary branches. He had great literary tastes and among his collection were works of all the writers of English classics; from which he could quote extensively. He make a special study of history and was widely known as a critic of modern history.

At age fifteen Mr. Jester began writing for the press, and these contributions were continued up until within a few months of his death. Among the latter subjects of his contributions were articles advocating "prohibition" for Kent County.

He was connected with the "Beacon," the first paper published in Milford. Upon leaving there he pursued the same profession in New York State; later returning to Kent County and connecting himself with the "News and Advertiser."

On July 13, 1863 Mr. Jester enlisted in Company I, 7th Delaware Infantry but was mustered out a few weeks later without seeing field service.

Mr. Jester also taught for many years in various rural schools including Kirby's school and was a promoter of many district debates, in which he always enjoyed the opportunity to participate.

He was prominent in political affairs, being a pronounced Republican, but would vote for a candidate of the opposition if he felt the candidate was a stronger man; putting the country's good above that of the party.

Mr. Jester was a loyal member of the Milford Neck Church, a Methodist Episcopal Church, in which he held many offices. He was a great student of the Bible and his depth of insight into the scriptures was a thing of beauty.

Isaac was married to Eliza Webb Donovan on April 26, 1867. Of their four children only one, George Henry, survived childhood. George made his home in Milford Neck near School 44. Isaac's wife, Eliza passed away on August 30, 1873. At the time of his death, from a heart attack on July 26, 1912, Isaac was living with his son, George.

Just before his death Mr. Jester was writing a book of biographical sketches of prominent Kent countians which was never completed. His departure created a vacancy in the neighborhood which was never filled.

ISAAC R. JESTER

1907

COURTESY OF MILFORD CHRONICLE

May 24, 1907

At the time of which we are writing the family of Ex-Governor Charles Polk perhaps was the most prominent of any in Milford Neck. He was a man of handsome physique and in manners and training a veritable type of the old school gentleman, and one of the most graceful horseback riders the writer ever knew. Surrounded by all the comforts and luxuries of life, and a family of eight children, educated and refined, his was an ideal home. As a factor in the affairs of state his usefulness was almost without limit. He had been President of the convention that framed the Constitution of 1831, a work that remained unchanged for sixty years, several times a member of the Legislature and twice Governor of the State of Delaware. Again, in 1843 Governor Cooper appointed him Register of Wills for Kent County which office he held for five years. When his lifelong friend, the Hon. John M. Clayton, entered the Cabinet of President Taylor in 1849 he promptly appointed Mr. Polk Collector of the Port of Wilmington, the duties of which he performed through the Taylor-Filmore administration. He died in 1857, honored and respected by all who knew him. After the death of his father, William A. Polk, the oldest son, became manager of the farm, a plantation of more than a thousand acres. Like his father William A. Polk was a man of sterling qualities. He too, was frequently called to positions of trust and honor in his county and state all of which he filled with strict fidelity. Another son John Purnell Polk held a clerkship at Washington for more than forty years. But two of the children of Governor Polk are now living; Mr. John O. Truitt, of Milford and Dr. Charles G. Polk, of Philadelphia. The farm is now the property of William I. Simpson who, since his ownership, has made very great improvements.

We will next mention the family of Elias Primrose. Mr. Primrose was a portly old gentleman of a very determined and pronounced character, blunt in his expression but generally admired. He was a consistent member of the M.E. Church and for years a class-leader. He owned and lived on the farm now owned by Mrs. James S. Hudson. He had a family of grown-up children. Two sons, Thomas and William had left the homestead to seek their fortunes in the "Sunny South." John W. was married and settled on the adjoining farm. Theodore, the youngest, was at home with his parents. Mr. Primrose died in Milford about 1854.

The adjoining farm then owned by Mr. Causey but now by Robert H. Williams, Esq., was tenanted by William Torbert a very industrious hard working farmer, with a family of grown-up boys. Few men were neater farmers than he.

On the farm now occupied by James Maloney and now owned by Robert H. Williams, resided John W. Primrose who during the excitement following the discovery of gold in 1848 sold out and started for California, went as far as Philadelphia. His enthusiasm abated however, he returned, removed to Milton and later died there. The farm owned by John Davis was purchased by his late father, James Davis, about 1843 to which he removed from the farm owned by Hon. Peter F. Causey, now the property of the heirs of the late Joshua Bennett. These farms have been improved more than one hundred per cent, in productiveness, since that time, and more than that amount in appearance by the erection of handsome and commodious buildings.

The track known as the "Big Stone" farm was owned by John Steward and tenanted by James Thompson who afterward moved to the Potter farm in the northern part of Milford Neck; except for grandchildren none of his descendants are now living. Situated on the south side of the Polk farm was the farm of Charles Jester which is still in possession of one of his sons. This farm had the misfortune to pass through the ordeals of life interest of his widow, controlled by her second husband and consequently was not much improved during her life time.

June 7, 1907

Adjoining the Polk farm on the north was a tract of land of about six hundred acres in a single farm. It was purchased by the late Joshua Bennett of Sussex county, who with his family took possession in 1843. Mr. Bennett's family consisted of three sons and three daughters, all nearly grown. He and his wife were well advanced in years. After his death in 1846 the farm became property of two of his sons, John and Joshua, who divided it as nearly equal as possible, the elder brother taking the part having the buildings. The land accepted by Joshua Bennett had no buildings, except a single story, one roomed house, in which he began housekeeping. Mr. Bennett was a "Hustler" in the full acceptation of the term; he engaged in farming and stock raising, and although live stock was of a nominal value at that time he was eminently successful. He has the distinction of being the first man in the Milford Neck to sell a horse for one hundred dollars. After a few years he divided his land into two farms, erected new buildings and so improved them that one would produce more that the entire tract had done, ten to twelve years before. He reared a family of nine children, all of whom are citizens of this community. Mr. Bennett has effectually answered the question; "Does Farming Pay?" and is now at the ripe age, enjoying the fruits of his early labors; a worthy example that other young men can well afford to follow. John Bennett also made two farms of his part of the estate, which after his death in 1862 and the death of his widow, who married David K. Watson, became the property of his two sons, Joshua S. and John W. John W. Bennett sold his farm to William Allen; since Allen's death it has changed ownership repeatedly, but has not changed in appearance. The dwelling house, except for the wear and waste of time, has an exact resemblance of sixty-five years ago. It is now owned by David W. Hall. Joshua S. Bennett's farm has been more fortunate in its management and is kept abreast of the times in modern improvements.

Adjoining the above tract on the north is the "Buck" farm, now the property of John W. Hall of Frederica. It was formerly owned by James S. Buckmaster, who was a candidate for Governor in 1858, and was defeated by Dr. William Burton. After the failure of Mr. Buckmaster, in 1859, it was bought by Mr. Hall's father, who afterward became Governor. This farm was, for a number of years, tenanted by William Virdin, who by his industry and economy accumulated enough money to buy a large tract of land, abutting the Murderkill River. He finally located in Frederica, where he died at an advanced age. The "Buck" farm, under its present ownership, has been greatly improved both in buildings and fertility, and is now one of the most productive in this section. It is now occupied by Jessie Sharp, a practical up to date farmer.

Next in order is the land of Nathaniel Luff. It contained about six hundred acres and was in two farms, but is now in three. On one of these Mr. Luff and his family lived. He was a stout, thick set man, weight about 200 pounds avoirdupoise, and shrewd business man with more than an ordinary fund of common sense. He was an inveterate talker, and cared but little in what manner his expressions were delivered. His wife was a devout Christian lady and one of the kindest and most motherly women the writer ever knew. The Luff homestead is now the property of William H. Bennett. Mr. Luff's family consisted of a wife, four sons and two daughters, he also had a son and daughter, John and Margaret, by a former wife. Nathaniel P. Luff, his oldest son by the second wife, engaged in the mercantile business, and became one of the most enterprising and successful business men of his time in lower Kent County. Caleb was associated with his brother in business for several years. Joshua was a cabinet maker and undertaker of the first order, but he died before he reached the meridian of life. Joseph, the youngest, lost his life by drowning in an unused well when a boy of less than six years of age. Anna and Susan married and located in Chicago and Philadelphia respectively. After the death of Mrs. Luff, Mr. Luff married his third wife, who died in little more than a year. He then married a fourth, by whom he had three children, Hester, Mary, and Charles. Mr. Luff died in Frederica at an advanced age; his fourth wife surviving him.

June 21, 1907

The farm adjoining the Luff homestead, also the property of Mr. Luff, was tenanted by Joshua McGonigal, an elderly gentleman with a family of children all nearly grown. His children were Samuel D., Rebecca married to Thomas Postles, Isaac, William, Mary, Joshua and John. Robert located in Greensborough, Md., embarked in the mercantile and grain trade and died there in 1851 leaving an estate of nearly one hundred thousand dollars. Isaac also opened a store at Luff's Corner, now owned by James A. Martin. He died in 1846. William engaged in farming and was quite successful. He purchased a farm in North Murderkill hundred upon which he lived many years. After the death of his father about 1841 Samuel D. McGonigal, with the help of his brothers, Joshua and John, conducted the farm; teaching school during the winter months. He had a fine education for that period, and was one of the best penman of his time. About 1847 the family removed to St. Jones Neck and afterwards to Dover. He died in Dover about 1889. John died in early manhood. Joshua McGonigal, now in his 84th year, lives in Dover, the only surviving member of that large and interesting family.

The farm on which the McGonigal family resided is now the property of Dr. J. M. Luff, of Felton, Del. During the lifetime of his father, the late N.P. Luff, it was improved and made one of the most desirable farms in Milford Neck. It is now in tenure of John R. Watkins.

On the south side of the road and opposite the Luff farm, is a tract of land, now the property of William H. French, then belonging to Thomas S. Temple, of Smyrna, Del. It was mostly in timber at that time; only about thirty acres being cleared, on which there stood a single story log house that would have done credit to the birthplaces of Lincoln and Garfield. It was sold to C. S. Watson and Brother about 1846, who worked the timber and in 1851 sold the land to Alfred Peet, of Philadelphia. Mr. Peet died shortly after moving to it, leaving a widow, two grown-up sons and a daughter as proprietors. The sons became dissatisfied in about a year and returned to Philadelphia. The mother and daughter remained on the property several years, having the land cultivated and keeping house together. Finally the daughter married Mr. French and he became proprietor. By dint of hard labor and economy he has made himself and family a neat and comfortable home.

At the west end of this tract is the hamlet of Thompsonville. The M. E. Church at this place has a history. The old church before described as being used for a school room, had outlived its usefulness, and it was necessary to build a new one but the people at that time did not think themselves equal to the task, financially.

The winter on 1841-2 was one of unusual severity. The accumulation of snow in the valley of the Schuykill was immense; the breaking up of which almost devastated the entire valley. Villages were almost annihilated. Mill yards and lumber wharfs were swept of their contents which found its way into the Delaware River and finally to the western shore of the bay. From Murderkill Cove to Mispillion Point was one continuous stretch of floating lumber. White pine and hemlock lumber of almost any dimensions was to be found in the partly stranded, partly floating mass. Thousands of feet of this lumber was carried ashore and piled on the beach by the natives. Everybody had lumber to contribute to the church if they had not money. The money market at that time was so limited that ten cent pieces were scarcer that silver dollars are today. Immediately after the drift of lumber a building committee was organized for a new church and Elias Primrose was placed at the head and the work of construction pushed so rapidly that early in 1843 it was ready for dedication. It was a frame structure of 26 x 30 feet, 18 1/2 feet high with side and end galleries and would seat an audience of 250 persons. The dedication took place in June 1843, the sermon being preached by the Reverend Henry White, D. D., Presiding Elder. Perhaps the success of this enterprise was due more to the indomitable energy of Rev. William Conly, preacher in charge, than to any other individual . A little previous to this he had succeeded in having built the Brick Church in the town of Milford at the corner of Third and North Streets. The M.E. Church in Milford Neck has been the place of worship for sixty-four consecutive years. In 1873 it was enlarged and remodeled to meet the requirements of the congregation. those that have preached in its pulpits are various and many, one of whom was the venerable and eccentric "Billy Barnes."

JAMES H. WEBB, JR.
Courtesy of Mrs. Sarah Webb

22

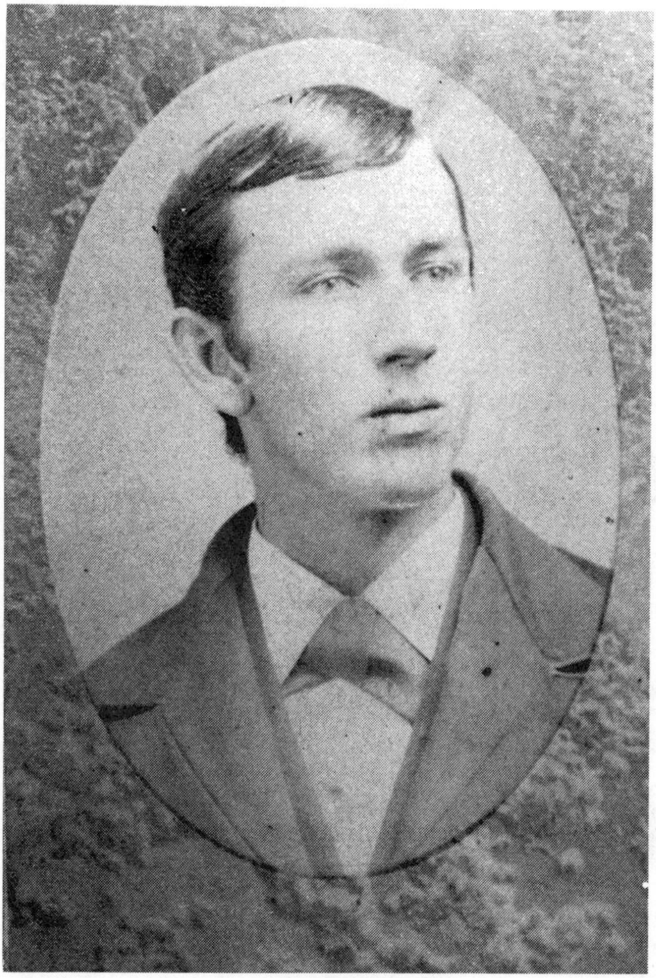

JAMES H. SIPPLE, JR.
Courtesy of Mrs. Sarah Webb

JULY 5, 1907

The farm located near the mouth of Murderkill River, now owned by Francis A. Webb, was one time the property of James Bell, and embraced the lands of James H. Webb, Jr., Charles Short and James H. Thomas in one farm. In the early forties it belonged to Dr. John Stradley of Frederica, and was tenanted by George W. Buckmaster, and afterwards by Jonathan N. Sipple - a progressive man of sterling qualities. Through his efforts a public road was opened from the "Lowber Farm" to the M. E. Church , and finally across the entire section. He also was the first man to open a Sunday School in Milford Neck. With his family he moved to Murderkill Neck in about the year 1847. John W.C. Webb followed Mr. Sipple as a tenant for a few years, the bought the farm of Dr. Stradley for the sum of $8000; an enormous price at that time.

We now come to notice the "Sipple Homestead" adjoining the above tract. It was owned and occupied by Mrs. Lavina (Sipple) Flemming, a widow, who by her masculine energy managed to bring up her children - four sons and a daughter. Her oldest son, Thomas Sipple, chose the life of a sailor became a captain of marked ability in the coastwise trade, and lost his life; his vessel being wrecked along the coast during a terrible snowstorm. James D. Sipple, the second son, continued with his mother until her death in 1847; after her death he bought the interests of the other heirs, became a successful farmer, prospered financially and died at 68 years of age; leaving an estate of $50,000. He was a man of steady habits, correct principles and unimpeached character. John Sipple and Caleb, his brothers, adopted the occupation of sailors and became master of seagoing vessels. John Sipple located in Milford, married there and reared a family. He was a careful, cautious man, and a general favorite of all with whom he was acquainted. Captain Caleb Sipple located in Greenwich, Conn., became a skillful navigator, engaged in the New England trade, in which he made money-but like most sailors, failed to save it. Miss Rachel, the sister, is the only surviving member of that family of five. James H. Sipple, son of James D. Sipple, now owns the farm which has been in possession of the family for more than a century.

On the south side of this, is a farm belonging to the "Potter Estate." Robert Mitten lived there in the early forties. He sold off his property and went to Michigan to grow up with the country; he was succeeded by William Thompson who remained until 1850, when he was succeeded by James Thompson, his father, who died there about 1872. Daniel A. Thompson was his father's successor for a number of years - the succession passing to William J. Thompson, who now occupies it. Thus it has been under the management of one family as renters for more than sixty years. Fifty years ago it contained about thirty acres of the most valuable red cedar timber, probably east of the Alleghany Mountains.

The next place to be noticed is the farm of James H. Kirby, formerly the property of the Harrington heirs. It was bought by William Thompson who occupied it till his death in 1853. His widow disposed of the property, and with her children went to Michigan about a year afterwards. Several of the children grew up, prospered, and became prominent citizens of Berrien county, Michigan.

Next in order is what was then known as the Henry M. Ridgely Farm. It was then tenanted by Nathaniel Bowman who went West in 1843. He was succeeded by Dickerson M. Meredith who continued there for twenty-four years. Mr. Meredith deserves rather more than a mere passing notice. He was quaint and extraordinary.

His disposition was an intricate study; a combination of the lamb and the lion. His ideals were lofty. He was uncompromising in what he deemed the right; a true friend, a kind husband and a devoted father. He died at an advanced age. Green be his memory. The Ridgely farm was purchased about 1866 by John W. Kirby, which he very much improved by erecting dwelling, barn and other necessary buildings. Mr. Kirby spent the remainder of his life on this farm. He also purchased two other farms which will be described in the next number.

July 12, 1907

John W. Kirby bought the two adjoining farms. They were one time the property of Michael and Isaac Lowber. Michael Lowber was a member of the Society of Friends, and died in Camden, Delaware, about 1861. After his death the farm was bought by James Postles, who built a new dwelling house and barn and otherwise improved it. The first man to occupy this farm as a tenant since my recollection was Henry Davis, a genial old gentleman with a large family of grown-up boys, the result of his first marriage, all of whom died in succession except the oldest, with that terrible disease, diphtheria, which was then called "black tongue fever." He had been some time married to his second wife, who was then mother of four children. None of this family is now living except William E. Davis, Esq., of Frederica, and Mrs. Major Harrington, of Brown's Neck. This farm is now occupied by one of Mr. Kirby's sons, Alexander Kirby.

The other Lowber farm, known as the "Brick House Farm," has on it the oldest dwelling house in this section, perhaps in lower Delaware; it having been built in 1733, its walls having stood "Time's corroding touch" for nearly two centuries. Traditional history describes it as having been built by a Swede by the name of Robinson. Sixty years ago it was very different in appearance from what it is now, especially the external architecture. It was built in the reign of George II, fifty years before the United States became a nation. This property, containing more than 200 acres, was bought in the decade of the forties by Reuben Bowman, at the nominal sum of $1,000. Here he made considerable improvement, flourished for a while, sold out and went to Wilmington. From Wilmington he emigrated to Missouri on the eve of the Civil War, there espoused the Union cause and has not been heard from since the breaking out of hostilities. Nevertheless he had one redeeming trait -- he was patriotic. This farm at present is occupied by another of Mr. Kirby's sons, Schuyler C. Kirby.

The next farm lying along the Murderkill River was owned by John W. Hall, a young businessman of Frederica. It was tenanted by Samuel Harris, who died there in the early forties, leaving a widow and two small children. Samuel, the son, was brought up by his uncle, Benjamin P. Needles. This farm at that time was not very remunerative. Mr. Hall, about 1850, bought the farm of 150 acres, lying on the opposite side of the road, having much valuable timber on it. This farm had been held by John Williams by virtue of his wife's dower, it being the property of her first husband. When his children reached their majority, it was bought by Mr. Hall, who cut the timber, cleared the land, and otherwise improved it; adding it to the other, he made a large and valuable farm. It was occupied for a number of years by Joseph French, one of the most industrious farmers of his time. It is now owned by John W. Hall, Jr., and tenanted by David Stevenson. Mr. Williams with his family went West and settled in Michigan near Niles.

The farm next above on the river now belonging to John Sipple, was the property of William T. Masten who lived on it with his three sons, Hesakiah, William and Clement. Mr. Masten was a very industrious and economical man, and accumulated a little fortune. His brother, John R.T. Masten (he spelled his name Masden) was a school teacher of that day. His education was fair, but his methods of teaching were antiquated, and his mode of discipline would not now by tolerated; and many a youth of his time had a mournful recollection of the way he taught "the young lad how to shoot.: He was a half-brother to the Rev. Charles P. Masden of national lad fame, than whom no other members of the Masten family repudiated the family name.

We are now at what was known as the "Coal's Shoal Farm" on the Murderkill River, containing 200 acres or more, owned by Aaron Bowman. He was a large portly man of fine appearance and to some extent a leading man in the community, and at the time considered a man of means. He built a store-house and embarked in the mercantile business in addition to his farming. He seemed successful for a while, but finally became victim to his own benevolence; sold his land to William Virden, his brother-in-law, and went to Wilmington. It now comprises two farms, one owned by Thomas Virden, the other by William Z. Hall. Mr. Hall has very much improved his farm by erecting commodious buildings.

July 19, 1907

The large tract of land situated on the Murderkill River above the Cole's Shoal Farm, comprising 500 acres or more and embraced in one farm, was one time the homestead of William Walker, a wealthy and prominent citizen of Milford Neck in his day and generation. Besides the plantation on which he lived, he owned a farm near Frederica, now known as the "Bye Farm." He also owned slaves, one of which, Peter Walker, a stout athletic colored man, lived to an extreme age. His master gave him his freedom and provided a home for him on his land during his life time; he survived his master about thirty years. Mr. Walker died about fifty-eight years of age, leaving a widow and one daughter. The daughter married the late Daniel C. Godwin, then a prominent young businessman of Milford, who became manager of the property. Mr. Godwin, subsequently, converted the land into two farms and otherwise improved it. About 1859 he embarked in peach culture, and at one time had the largest orchard in lower Kent county. Mr. Godwin died in 1895 at the age of about seventy-nine years. His widow, Mrs. Sarah Walker Godwin, survives him in her ninetieth year. After the death of Mr. Godwin, her son, Dr. William F. Godwin, of Reistertown, Md., became proprietor of the farms. They are tenanted by Matthew Mitten and James P. Thomas, two progressive up-to-date young farmers, and Dr. Godwin may congratulate himself upon his good fortune in making such a selection. Matthew F. Mitten, father of the present tenant, occupied one of these farms for a period of forty years. In point of character he was a model man; one of the best that Milford Neck ever possessed. Like Burn's father "his feelings leaned to virtues side." These farms are among the finest in Milford Neck and are very productive. Dr. Godwin keeps them in splendid condition, and justly takes pride in their neat appearance.

The next farm, formerly known as the "Molleston" Farm, was owned by Major Townsend, an eccentric old gentleman of Frederica, whose daughter, Mrs. James F. Sipple, became sole heir. It is a plantation of more than 500 acres, and at one time was owned by Henry Moleston, who was elected Governor in 1820 and died before being inaugurated. It became the property of Paris T. Carlisle in the early sixties. It has been tenanted by John W.C. Webb, George Henderson, Parrot Kirby, John Ericson, William C. Holland, John Raughley, Charles P. Taylor, George H. Davis and Joseph Perkins. Toward the close of the nineties, Mr. Carlisle's sons, Drs. Paris T. and Lester L. Carlisle, took charge and converted it into a dairy and stock farm. They also erected a large creamery plant which they managed for several years. Failing to realize as much as had been expected they abandoned the enterprise; the younger brother taking charge of the farm, which he now employs in the growth of grain, fruit and vegetables. Under the late management the value of the farm has been very much enhanced. It is a plot of land adapted to the growth of any product indigenous to this climate.

On the opposite side of the road, leading to Frederica, is the farm of James A. Martin. It was at one time the property of the late Nathaniel Luff, and was called "Luff's Corner." For a while a store was kept there. It was bought by John Martin, of Sussex County, who moved to it in 1842. Mr. Martin was a quiet, law abiding citizen, and a consistent Christian gentleman, honored by all who knew him. He died suddenly of heart failure in 1858, while engaged in thrashing grain, not much beyond the meridian of life. He left a widow and three children, John, his oldest son, the issue of his first marriage; Richard, his son by his second wife, was an intelligent youth, studied medicine, became a doctor and settled in Pennsylvania; James A. grew up on the farm, and has made farming his principal occupation. He has served in the Levy Court, also in the Legislature, and perhaps, would have filled other important places of public trust and honor, had it not been that his usefulness was circumscribed by becoming extremely hard of hearing. Mr. Martin has been eminently successful as a farmer. He has bought an adjoining tract and how has a model farm.

July 26, 1907

The tract of land adjoining James A. Martin's farm on the east, in the early forties, was the property of Lewis Passmore, of Philadelphia, and contained between three and four hundred acres. It was fully timbered and Mr. Passmore had it worked into ship timber, bark, staves and cord wood. Mr. Passmore was a very large man, his weight being more than 350 pounds. The writer remembers on one occasion, when he came to our home on business he seated himself on two chairs, being afraid to risk an ordinary one. Sometime afterwards he sold the farm to Job Ridgway, an old Quaker gentleman, who came with his family from Philadelphia to the farm. Himself and three sons, Jacob, Charles and Willet, two of whom were nearly grown, cultivated the farm. Mr. Ridgway was unsuccessful as a farmer, became involved financially and a few years afterward was sold out by the sheriff and returned to Philadelphia, "a wiser and sadder man." One of Mr. Ridgway's sons, Jacob, became a prominent man in the Keystone State and prospered. He became a member of the Pennsylvania Legislature; became wealthy, and founded what was once Ridgway Park. At the sheriff sale the farm was purchased by Samuel Warren, maternal grandfather of the present owner, John W. Hall. Of late years it has been very much improved.

The next property adjoining belongs to the heirs of the late Daniel A. Thompson, and at my earliest recollections was the property of his grandmother, Mrs. Margaret (Kelley) Thompson. It was known as the Kelley tract. The first family living there within the recollection of the writer was that of William Redden who went West.

About the year 1842 there was a regular exodus of the people of this vicinity for the West. The State of Michigan had but recently become a State. Many men ambitious for a wider field of opportunities than was afforded here sold out their belongs except those which could be packed in wagons and began a journey toward the setting sun. The families of Thomas Powell, Nathaniel Bowman, Petter Ellis, Nehemiah Macklin, George Abbott, William Redden, Robert Mitten, Morgan Williams and later John Williams, James Master, Benjamin Parsons, Elias Parsons and Mrs. Mary Thompson left for the land of promise. Those who went to Michigan settled in Cass and Berrian counties in the southwestern part of the State and is still known as the Delaware settlement. Very many of the descendants of those early settlers are citizens of that locality and have helped to develop and make Michigan one of the leading states of the nation.

The year 1842 was a year of incidents. A great commotion was started in Milford Neck by the preaching of false prophets called Second Adventist or Millerites. A crank by the name of Miller being of a mathematical turn of mind had figured that on the 24th day of June 1842 the world would be destroyed. For a time great excitement prevailed among the weak minded and credulous. But the commotion soon subsided and people again became rational.

The farm on the opposite side of the road belonged to Winlock Hall, a large land holder and wealthy man, who bequeathed it to his grandson, Winlock H. Thomlinson, then in his boyhood. After Mr. Thomlinson became at age he erected new buildings and cleared more of the land and otherwise improved it, making a very desirable property. It is now the property of Robert J. Meredith. Winlock H. Thomlinson was a sterling qualities; kind, accommodating and generous to a fault. He died in 1864 in the prime of his manhood, scarcely 35 years of age.

> Oh, why has worth so short a date,
> While villains ripen gray with time.

The next farm was the home of William D. Masten, who reared a family of six children -- four sons and two daughters, none of whom live in this community. His wife was a kind motherly old lady, as nearly faultless as humanity is capable of being. The children when grown up went to different localities. Two settled in Wilmington, two went West and two others are now living near Bridgeville, Delaware.

August 9, 1907

The farm situated on the east of the William D. Masten farm, and now owned by Joshua Bennett, Jr., was once the property of Thomlinson Parsons, and it contained about two hundred acres. It was subsequently divided into three parts; one becoming the property of his son, Benjamin Parsons; one was bought by Williams Hall, and the third was the dower of his widow. Afterwards it descended to Mr. Hall and the heirs of Benjamin Parsons, jointly, William Thompson, who married the daughter of Mr. Parsons, became proprietor of her share of the property. About 1844 he sold it to Wm. Saxton, who occupied it till the Mexican War, when he bought the "Tub Mill," so that, as a miller, he would be exempt from service -- if there should be a draft for soldiers. Mr. Saxton's devotion to his family entirely destroyed his patriotism. On the part belonging to Mr. Hall lived a widowed lady, Mrs. Hester Ann, and her brother, Alexander Spence. Her son, Thomas Dorrel, was without doubt one of the most wayward youths Milford Neck every produced. After the death of Mr. Hall, his interest was bought by Mr. Bennett's father, Joshua Bennett, Sr. He finally bought the part formerly owned by Mr. Thompson and converted it into one farm. It is now one of the most desirable and most productive farms in this part of Kent County.

On the opposite side of the road, now owned by John S. Reynolds of Frederica, was once the home of John Thompson; a man, stern, inflexible and somewhat arbitrary in disposition, who aspired to leadership in the community. He was a man of some ability and not without redeeming traits of character. At one time he was engaged in keeping store, and was quite successful. In 1848 he was elected to the Levy Court, and performed his duty in office as faithfully as any man ever sent to that body from Milford Hundred. He had a family of five children, three of whom are dead; the other two, if living, are somewhere in the Western States.

The tract adjoining the Thompson property on the east, now embracing the home of Joseph C. Bennet and the hamlet of Thompsonville, was one time the property of Lewis Passmore, and was sold to Nathan Livingston in 1849. It is now worth many thousands of dollars.

About a half mile south of the M.E. Church, on the road leading to Milford, was the home of Townsend Meredith. The farm was the maiden property of his wife who was his third matrimonial venture. They had a family of seven children, all of whom grew up to man and womanhood in this vicinity, except James, who was drowned at the Mordington Mills when a boy. William Henry acquired a fair education in the Common Schools of the time; read medicine and finally became a practicing physician and located at Smithville, Md. John T. Meredith and his brother, Daniel, managed the farm until the death of their mother, when it was sold to Thomas Vicory. Mr. Vicory sold it to Joseph Wyatt, and he sold it to David Postles it was bought by James D. Sipple, and has remained in the Sipple family. It is now a neat well kept farm, producing abundant crops. So much has it been improved, that it would scarcely be recognized by persons who had not seen it for fifty years.

On the opposite side of the road is the farm of Charles Kirby. It was one time the property of Winlock Hall, who died in the early forties, leaving it with two other farms to his grandson, John A. Hall. At the time he came at age his heritage was worth ten thousand dollars; it did not require ten years to find the bottom of it. Adjoining this tract was another farm belong to Mr. Hall, which he also bequeathed to his grandson, John A. Hall. It is now the property of David B. Hall -- another grandson to whom he left nothing. David B. Hall grew up to be an industrious, hard working man. He accumulated enough in a few years to purchase the farm when it was sold from his brother. He has erected new buildings, cleared and improved the land, and now has a comfortable and pleasant home.

August 30, 1907

South of the farm of David B. Hall, on the road leading to Milford, is a small farm, once the property of the late John Livingston. It formerly contained about sixty acres, but was divided into two parts, so that his sons, Nathan and Thomas, could each be provided with a home after the death of their father. Thomas built on his part, a one story house about the year 1843, which he occupied for two years, when he became afflicted with the 'don't-have-to-work" principle; sold out to Isaac Jester and located in Milford, supposing it to be an asylum for the lame and lazy. Thomas Livingston was a mathematical genius; he could give the correct solution of almost any problem, by a process of reasoning entirely his own, which he was unable to explain to any one else. Mr. Jester lived on the property for nearly fifty years, during which time he reared a family of just one dozen children. He died in the nineties, about eighty six years of age; his widow ninety years of age still survives him. The property is now owned by Peter L. Lofland of Milford. The other part, intended for Nathan, was occupied by his father, John Livingston, until his death in 1854, meanwhile his son Nathan had gone to Michigan and located near Ann Arbor. After a few years, all knowledge of his whereabouts was lost. The property was occupied by the widow of John Livingston for several years. After her death it was in tenure of John M. Bennett who had married her daughter. Finally Mr. Bennett quit the property, and it became tenantless and virtually without an owner. Later on in years the placed was captured on the principal of "squatter sovereignty" by John Foster Loper, who still occupies it. Mr. Loper was a Russian refugee, who fled his country during the Crimean War to avoid the conscription phase of the Czar, while the allied armies of England and France were battering the walls of Sebastopol. John Livingston was a quaint old gentleman and strikingly peculiar. He was said to be a direct descendant of one of the Hessian soldiers captured by Washington's Army at the Battle of Trenton.

Opposite the Livingston place, now owned by Edward Thomas, was the land of William Welch, familiarly known to every one as "Uncle Billy." Mr. Welch, in his early manhood, had been a seafaring man and was much given to the habit of spinning "yarns," for which the average sailor is proverbial. The writer, though but a boy at the time, distinctly remembers some of his sea stories that were very near miraculous. He was a man with a large fund of intelligence, gleaned mostly from his travels, which was interesting in the extreme, if taken with a moderate degree of allowance.

We are now at the farms of Edward R. Meredith, the front one of which was the property of George Beswick, who sold it to Mr. Meredith's father, Dickerson M. Meredith, and went West in the early forties. The other farm was the property of Mr. Beswick's sister, Mrs. Margaret Dennis, who finally sold it to Mr. Meredith. He erected buildings on the land, cleared and improved it. He now has two nice farms, all the results of his industry and economy.

The next tract of land south of Meredith's farm, and situated on each side of the road leading to Milford, known as the "Lowery land," was owned by Peter F. Causey and contained about two hundred acres. Mr. Causey sold it to William B. Gray in 1845, for the low price of four hundred and fifty dollars. Mr. Gray sold about three hundred dollars worth of timber from he land to Absolem Hill for four hundred dollars. He then sold twenty-six acres of the other half to Dickerson M. Meredith for seventy-five dollars, after which he was compelled to sell the remaining seventy acres to pay the purchase money. Mr. Hill erected buildings and otherwise improved it, so that his part became a nice, desireable property. He occupied it as a home for a number of years. After the death of Mr. Hill, int he division of his estate, it became the property of his widow, who has recently sold it for three thousand and three hundred dollars.

September 6, 1907

In our last article we gave a description of what was once the home of Absolem Hill; it is now our duty to say something of the man. Having previously purchased this tract of worn out land, which had been "turned out to a common," he built a house upon it in the latter part of 1853, and shortly after with his wife, whom he had recently married, took possession. With his land denuded of all valuable timber, and that part which had been arable was almost a barren waste and almost as unproductive as the Desert of Sahara, except for the presence here and there of scraggly pines, cedars and scrub oaks, it must be admitted that his prospect for eminent success did not seem very flattering. But Mr. Hill was a strong athletic young man, possessed of industry and a vast amount of "push," and his wife also was equally persevering. Fortunately, however for Mr. Hill and his poor land, that period was in the palmy days of Peruevian guano; it revolutionized the farming industry in this section and by dint of hard labor and liberal application of guano he succeeded in clearing his land and producing generous crops, and in less that ten years he had a paying farm, showing conclusively what may be achieved by unflinching industry and perseverance. Early in 1869 Mr. Hill bought the property near the M.E. Church, now Thompsonville, but did not occupy it personally for several years. Finally, he moved to his late purchase and embarked into the mercantile business and was quite successful. He died in 1888, aged about sixty-three years, leaving a widow and three grown up children - one son and two daughters. He was an honorable, upright man, a consistent member of the M.E. Church and respected by the community in which he lived. His son, George T. Hill, is a thrifty, well-to-do farmer of Milford Neck. His older daughter became the wife of the late Mark G. Lofland; his younger daughter became the wife of Dr. James G. Stanton, of Milford.

That part of the Lowery tract lying on the opposite side of the road, and owned by John H. Hall at the present, was held by Mr. Gray for a few years; when it was purchased by George C. Hering, of Philadelphia, and occupied by his brother, Abner Herring. As a farmer Mr. Hering was not a success, but he was a model of politeness and in manner of a close imitation of Lord Chesterfield. While in the possession of Mr. Gray it was but little improved. He was one of those unfortunate characters who could not stand prosperity. Although he had stumbled into a bargain in real estate that would have made many a man independent he failed utterly to embrace the opportunity. His worst besetment was his inordinate thirst for the beverage "that inebriates but does not cheer." Such was the life and character of William B. Gray; that after a long and unsuccessful life he died in an institution of charity. On the memory of this unfortunate man let the mantle of charity be spread! After the death of George C. Hering the land was sold to a Mr. Knipe, Pennsylvanian, who in time sold it to John W. Kirby, who held it but a short time and sold out the Elnathan Smith. Mr. Smith occupied the property for awhile then moved to Milford, leasing it to Clarence Hopkins & Bro., who set it in peach trees. After the expiration of the lease it was bought by the present owner, John H. Hall.

Immediately back of the last named tract is the farm of Robert G. Richards, containing seventy-eight acres. It was bought by his father , William H. Richards, about 1831 for two hundred and forty dollars. He reared a family of nine children and died in 1809 aged more that eighty-four years. He was a quiet unobtrusive man, of whom but a few persons could justly speak evil.

The next place to be noticed is "Hering's Corner," now the property of William G. Hering of Milford, It was for a long time the home of Samuel Hering, his father. Samuel Hering was, without doubt, one of the most persevering and hard working men that ever lived in this community. He was regarded as a practical farmer of his day, but was one of those men whom Dame Fortune seemingly fails to reward. he died in 1874 aged about seventy-six years.

September 13, 1907

Adjoining the "Herring's Corner" property on the east is the farm of John C. Clifton. Previous to 1843 it was a tract of worn out land belonging to Curtis B. Beswick, who sold it to Daniel C. Clifton for a small sum; land at that time not bringing on the market beyond three dollars per acre. Mr. Clifton built a house upon it and began the routine of life, which at that time meant hard labor and rigid economy. In a few years he had improved his land so that it produced a support for his family, which consisted of seven members. He was a careful pains-taking man, and one of those who "make haste slowly." In a few years, though not as wealthy as some others, he was living independently as any man of his time. He died in 1884, at the age of 72 years, leaving a widow and three grown children to survive him. His brother, Skyrain Clifton, was of a roving disposition but finally located in Massachusetts - the land of "Baked Beans and Boston Culchaw." Mr. Daniel C. Clifton's children were: Sallie, who married Nemiah Cole, a young farmer of Milford Neck, now residing in Milford; Angeline, who married James H. Kirby, an industrious and thrifty mechanic of Milford Neck; they reside on their farm, Mr. Kirby having adopted that occupation; John C., the son, having received a good education, taught in the free schools for a number of years. After the death of his father, John C. Clifton bought the interests of his sisters in the homestead, erected a new dwelling house and otherwise improved it; it is one of the best located tracts of land in Milford hundred and is now occupied by Mr. Clifton's son, Harvey. John C. Clifton resided in milford and is a bookkeeper for the form of Draper, Davis & Co.

To the east of, and adjoining the Clifton land, is the farm of Herman Abbott, D.D.S., of Philadelphia. It was formerly the home of the late Nathaniel B. Thomas. Mr. Thomas bought the tract of unimproved land containing about seventy acres, in the early fifties. He erected suitable buildings upon it and began to clear and cultivate the land. Though laboring under difficulties, he succeeded in building up a comfortable home for himself and family, which he occupied for many years. Finally, under the stress of financial embarrassment, superinduced by entering too deeply into the political arena, he succumbed into liquidation - by which he lost his home. It was purchased by Rynear Williams, who sold it to William L. Abbott, who sold it to the late John W. Hall, of Frederica and during whose ownership it was improved by repairing the dwelling and erecting new out houses. Mr. Hall finally sold it to Herman Abbott,who still holds it.

Nathaniel B. Thomas was a man of many parts - he had failings as other men, but he was possessed of many commendable and redeeming traits, which went a long way toward retrieving the objectionable features of his character. He made enemies but he made many friends, whose friendship was lasting. Viewed from the better side of his disposition, he was an alright man; charitable, kind-hearted and generous to a fault. He was one of those men whose charity began at home, but did not stop thee; it was bestowed on others, often to his own injury. He provided well for his own house hold, and contributed unsparingly to outside charities, very often to an extent that taxed his ability. he was a member of the M. E. Church for the major portion of his life, and a diligent worker in the Sunday School; in which he had an abiding faith in its efficiency to elevate the rising generation to a higher plane of citizenship. Mr. Thomas died in 1889, aged sixty-nine years. His widow and twelve grown children survive him.

The land adjoining Dr. Herman Abbott's farm on the north, now the property of Aaron H. Thomas, was at one time the home of John Thomas, his grandfather, who died at an advanced age in the early forties. He is remembered by but few persons in this vicinity. After the death of the old gentleman, his son, George Thomas, bought out the interest of the other heirs and it became his home for a period of nearly fifty years.

September 29, 1907

(I am informed by Mr. William Abbott, who has recently returned from an extended tour to the Pacific states, that he is the real owner of the farm described in our article of last week; that he and not his son Dr. Abbott bought it of Mr. Hall. We cheerfully make this correction and apologize to our readers in general and Mr. Abbott in particular for our misapprehension of the fact. It is our province to state facts concisely without injustice to any and we hope Mr. Abbott will accept this correction in the same spirit of serenity is made.)

We now come to notice Mount Pleasant the original homestead of the Beswick family. It formerly was in one plantation, situated on the south side of the Public road and extending from Fishing Creek to Beaver Dam and containing about five hundred acres. It is beautifully located on the Mispillion river, and is seen at its best advantage from that stream. It is now in three separate farms; one the property of John W. Herring, and tenanted by George R. Johnson; one by James H. Evans; one by John Hammond. The one owned by Mr. Herring was the home of his grandfather, Curtis B. Beswick. Mr. Beswick spent nearly the entire period of his life, on the farm, and was regarded as one of the most progressive farmers of his time; he was a plain, unostentious man and had a way of saying plain things very plainly. Next to Ex-Governor Charles Polk he was one of the most prominent men in the community,. He was a staunch supporter of Free Schools, and always took a deep interest in popular education. He reared a family of four children - two sons and two daughters all of whom grew up to be highly esteemed and useful citizens. Mr. Beswick died in 1880, at the ripe age of eighty-four years leaving an estate valued at thirty thousand dollars.

The farm now in tenure of James H. Evans, was formerly a part of the home property of Curtis B. Beswick. After his death, in the division of his real estate, it was given to his son Robert J. Beswick as his share. Esquire Beswick erected extensive new buildings upon it, improved the land and fashioned it into one of the most valuable as well as most beautiful farms in this section. It is now owned by Mrs. John Hammond and her sister Miss Anna P. Beswick. The farm on which John Hammond resides was for many years the home of William P. Beswick. It is a fine farm, nicely located and very productive with all the necessary buildings required. After the death of Mr. Beswick, his family remained on the farm, until Mrs. Beswick's health became so impaired that she was no longer able to endure the worry of farm life she retired. She had erected a very substantial building as a home. It is built in English cottage style of colonial times, and is very conveniently arranged in all its apartments. It is a unique building located on one of the most picturesque spots in this part of the country, amid the singing of birds and blooming of flowers. William P. Beswick was a teacher in the public schools for nearly a quarter of a century. After he was married he engaged in farming but continued teaching as well for a number of years when he gave it up and directed his time entirely to the cultivation of his farm. In addition to agriculture he was engaged in horticulture and pomology in which he took great delight. He was a man of general intelligence and liberal views. He died in 1892, at the age of sixty-four years. Robert J. Beswick, his brother, was a man in some respects peculiar. He was a born financier. From his youth he evinced a strong inclination to practice economy and save his earnings. While yet a young man he began a system of investments that yielded large returns. Whenever opportunity afforded he invested his surplus earnings in stocks and bonds of large paying capacity in form of dividends. In a few years and at the time when the vessel property was paying large dividends, he began to invest in vessels suited to the coastwise trade. These investments brought him large returns. He also made purchases of real estate which he improved in a manner to make it paying property. He was a shrewd business man and one of the best financiers Milford Neck ever produced - he was more than that - He was one of the Creators noblest works - an honest man. He died in 1907 aged seventy-two years.

October 18, 1907

The tract of land situated on the south side of the road, and extending from Beaver Dam to King's Causeway, was formerly the property of the late Winlock Hall and was in two farms. Mr Hall is remembered as an elderly gentleman with very prominent features. He was a man of considerable importance in his day, and one of the largest land holders of Milford Neck; owning several farms at the time of his death. He died at an advanced age, about the year 1841, leaving three sons to survive him. To William, his oldest and most trustworthy son, he left the greater portion of his wealth. To his second son, Draper, he left a home and a yearly income during his life. To his youngest son John he left one farm, with an additional bequest of money. His grandsons, Winlock H. Tomlinson and John A. Hall, were each given a farm. After his father's death William Hall, who had become of the homestead as well as the adjoining farm, assumed control of the property. By virtue of his father's will he was guardian of the two grandsons, Winlock H. Tomlinson and John A. Hall. Shortly after the death of his father he bought of his brother, John M. Hall, the farm which he inherited, situated on the Beauamp-Brig creek and about one mile North of the M.E. Church, containing one hundred and fifty-six acres. It was leased to different individuals for a period of nearly thirty years.

Mr. Hall planted a large orchard of apple trees; consisting of arch, cider, grixon, russet and cain apples; about the only varieties then known in this section. When this orchard came into profit Mr. Hall utilized the crops by converting them into cider and brandy. He continued the business of distilling brandy, which had been profitably conducted by his father, for a number of years and finally abandoned it entirely.

He occupied the farm situated on the Mispillion River, which he received from his father, for nearly forty years, during which time he was a prominent and useful man. He was honest and upright in all his business transactions, and merited and held the implicit confidence of the entire community. He died in 1870, in the sixty-eighth year of his age and it can truly be said of him, without fear of successful contradiction, his pocket never jingled with a dishonest dollar. In the settlement of the estate of William Hall, Dr. Thomas Cahall, administrator, sold all the real estate except the Daniel Mason tract of one hundred and fifty-six acres. His brother, John M. Hall, bought the home farm; his oldest son, John Wesley Hall bought the adjoining farm and Joshua Bennett, Sr., bought the Parson's tract. In 1873 William E. Hall, one of the heirs, obtained a decree of court for the division of the remaining land. The commissioners appointed by the court were: James Postles, William T. Masten, James D. Sipple, John W. Kirby, and Issac R. Jester. With the assistance of James H. Postles, a skillful surveyor, the succeeded in making, as nearly as possible, an equitable division, giving to each of the six heirs an average of about twenty-eight acres. Charles, Henry and George sold theirs to Esquire James B. Davis, who cut the timber and sold the land to Maurice Mosley. Alexander David sold his share to Daniel Thompson, who converted it into a nice little farm. Maurice Mosely cleared the land, built upon it and made a valuable farm of about sixty acres. William E. Hall sold his to Gibson Walls for eight dollars per acre. Winlock B. Hall still holds his; he and his brother John Wesley being the only two that have any of the real estate formerly belonging to their ancestors. John Wesley Hall's farm contains about one hundred and twenty-five acres and is located on the Mispillion River; it is highly improved and very productive. The farm adjoining, formerly the homestead, is now the property of Edward S. Beswick. It is beautifully located on the Mispillion River and was formerly sold by the heirs of John M. Hall to Mr. Beswick's uncle, Robert J. Beswick.

November 8, 1907

Situated on the south side of the public road and adjoining the Winlock homestead is a tract of land now the property of Jehu Davis which one time was the property of John Surand. Mr. Surand lost his life attempting to swim the Mispillion River at Hickman's Landing. After his death his widow with her infant boy returned to her former home in Northern New Jersey. The boy grew up to manhood, acquired an education and became a successful minister of the Gospel. A number of years ago this writer met the Rev. Mr. Surand at Tompkin's Cove, Rockland County, N.J., where he was stationed as pastor. He made anxious inquiry after his birthplace and early childhood home. This farm which formerly contained about one hundred and sixty acres has been divided into two tracts one of which is owned by Dr. Robert Y. Watson of Milford. The one owned by Mr. Davis is now tenanted by Samuel Coverdale. It was susceptible of a high state of improvement and well adapted to the growth of grass and grain.

Adjoining this tract, and situated immediately on the broad Mispillion, is the banner farm of this section. It was once the home of the late Nathaniel Hickman. Mr Hickman was a remarkable genius and a very prominent man of his day and generation. He was a ship carpenter by trade and build several vessels, at his landing on the river. His remains rest in the family burial ground on the farm. he left a considerable estate and his minor son, John Hickman, became sole heir. John Hickman after reaching his majority, entered the firm of Gum, Hickman & Long, of Frankford, Sussex County Delaware, and embarked extensively in the mercantile business. He sold several parcels of his land and finally sold the homestead to the late Benjamin Henderson. After the death of Mr. Henderson, it was sold by his heirs to Andrew J. Maloney in the early seventies. At the time of Mr. Maloney's purchase, the farm was in deplorable condition. The buildings were dilapidated and tottering almost to their downfall; fences had been neglected and headlands and fence rows had become unsightly thickets of bramble and brushwood. He erected new and commodious buildings, reclaimed and improved the land and now has instead of almost barren waste, one of the most beautiful and excellent farms in this locality yielding immense crops of grain, grass, tomatoes, etc. This farm is conveniently situated on the Mispillion River; has an excellent landing, with a good public road leading thereto, at which the Steamer City of Milford touches four times a week. Mr. Maloney is justly proud of his achievement in the development of this property; he recently refused an offer of $5700 for it as it is paying a revenue on more that $7000 per annum.

The adjoining farm was also formerly the property of the late Nathaniel Hickman and was sold in the decade of the fifties to John Townsend. After Mr. Townsend's death it was again sold, subject to his widow's dower, to James M. Cain, for a sum less than seven hundred dollars. Perhaps the cause of so small a realization on this sale, was that it was sold in 1861 after the opening of hostilities when the business of the country was paralyzed. After the death of Mr. Cain, about 1866, his widow remained on the farm. Her family consisted of four children - three sons and one daughter and her brother, Mr. Nehemiah Bennett, who managed the farm. By dint of heroic efforts and herculean exertions, Mrs. Cain succeeded in rearing her children and placing her farm on a paying basis. Of the four children, three of them have left the parental home and set up for themselves. Joshua, the oldest, like many ambitions young men, went west to grow up with the country. Nehemiah bought a farm and occupies it, half way between Frederica and Felton. Sallie became Mrs. George Reynolds of Milford. John still remains on the farm with his mother, who is past eighty years of age. Few women in this section deserve as much credit for the manner in which she has brought up her children and managed her affairs, as does Mrs. Cain.

October 15, 1907

Lying between the two Hickman farms was formerly a small farm belonging to Robert Maloney. Since 1840, it has been successively owned by Mr. Maloney, James Steele, Benjamin Ennis, Col. C. S. Watson and Mrs.. Mary B. Cain, who has since her ownership removed the buildings and incorporated it with her home property. The last tenant to occupy this property as a separate farm was Mr. John Maloney who died there in 1880, aged about 77 years. In the early forties Mr. Maloney lived on the Lower Hickman farm and continued there for a number of years. He reared an interesting family of six children all of whom lived to grow up respected citizens. Sarah the oldest married Truston Mason and died in Chester, Pa. a few years ago. William T. the oldest son, grew up one of the very best young men in the community. He located at Lebanon, Kent County, De., and died there. J. Andrew the second son, who was mentioned in our last article, grew up on the farm. Early in life he married and set up for himself. He possessed a large amount of native ability, an indomitable will of his own and has been eminently successful. Susan united her fortune with John W. Kirby in marriage and became one among the best wives and mothers. By their industry and economy they managed to accumulate a snug little fortune. She is living in Milford; quietly and pleasantly enjoying the fruits of her earlier toil. John R. Maloney is a well-to-do-farmer of Milford Neck and lives on one of the farms of Col. Robert H. Williams. His children are all grown and have left the parental board.

Caroline, the youngest daughter, married Joseph A. Clendaniel a worthy young man of this section. They went west about 1840 and settled in Wisconsin.

The Hickman farm now the property of A. J. Maloney and tenanted by Henry Tribbitt and his parents, was occupied in the decade of the forties by John Abbott at that time a little past the meridian of life. Mr. Abbott was a man of excellent traits of character and a typical old time gentleman. He has a family of three children, viz., William W., Eliza Jane, and Henry H. He trained his children up to habits of industry and respectability, the best legacy any parent can bestow. William W. Abbott quit the farm, learned the carpenters trade and located in Milford, where he died a few years ago. He was the parent of S. J. Abbott and Charles D. Abbott, of the firm of C. D. Abbott & Co. of Milford, Del., and of Mrs. Robert C. Hall of Saratoga, N.Y., Eliza Jane married Capt. Thomas Purnell, of Lebanon, who was drowned a number of years ago, in an attempted passage from the mainland to Cross Ledge Lightship of which he was master. She is now living with her son, John Purnell, on his farm near Milton. Henry H. Abbott for a while was a farmer. Subsequently, he abandoned that occupation and located in Milford, where he has resided for many years. He is a veteran of the Civil War, a member of the Grand Army of the Republic, and in 1902 was elected coroner of Kent County.

Following after Mr. Abbott, as a tenant, on the Hickman farm was Benjamin Dickerson who occupied it for a number of years. He was one of the most strangely peculiar individuals of this section. He was a good neighbor if cautiously approached but woe be to him who incurred his displeasure. His grandest hobby was the law; if he had known such authorities as Vattel, Blackstone, Coke of Littelton etc. as well as he knew the statutory law he would have been a giant. But he did not and 'thereby hangs a tale.' He was considered a fair farmer for his time. His family consisted of a wife and seven children, two sons and five daughters. Three of his daughters married farmers. Naomi married John R. Maloney, Eliza married John Wesley Hall, Adeline married Isaac M. Thomas. None of these are now living. Mary died in her youth; Caleb married and settled on a farm near Leipsic; John and Susan are still unmarried.

We now come to notice one of the farms of Col. Robert H. Williams, now in tenure of Walter Holleger. This farm adjoins the farm of Mrs. Mary Cain and is nicely located on the Public Road. It is well adapted to the growth of grass and grain, the proceeds of which are quite remunerative. For more than half a century it has been under the tenant system, during which time it has been managed by some excellent farmers. We should judge it to be a good farm to make money from the fact that several men have accumulated enough upon it to buy a farm of their own while living there.

November 29, 1907

The next farm to be described is also the property of Col. Robert H. Williams, which adjoins the one mentioned in our last article. It was formerly owned by the late Ex-Governor Causey, and was one of the four farms, constituting one unbroken block of about seventeen hundred acres. In the early fifties Mr. Causey sold this entire body of land to Thomas Catts and David C. Pennewill, successors to C. S.

Watson and Co., in the mercantile business. They made considerable outlay in the way of improvements. To use a very expressive if not classical phrase, they had "bitten off more than they could chew," and in the monetary crisis following the inauguration of President Buchanan, in 1857, went down under the weight of financial embarrassment. Mr. Causey was compelled to foreclose the mortgage and take the land. The partnership existing between Catts and Pennewill was dissolved. Mr. Catts locating in Yonker, N.Y., a picturesque little city on the eastern side of the Hudson River, where he died sometime in the sixties. Mr. Pennewill embarked in the Commission business to recoup his fortune.

On the opposite side of the public road is a small farm, the property of Charles Watkins, which was formerly a part of the Primrose tract. Since he has owned it he has made of it a comfortable home, where he enjoys life immensely, having sufficiency to satisfy his demands. He is one of the most independent men of this section. His father the late Eli R. Watkins of Milford was a resident of Milford Neck for a half century and here brought up his family of nine children - four sons and five daughters. Mr. Watkins was a man of unquestioned integrity his character almost without a spot or blemish. He died in the nineties about eighty years of age.

The next farm on the north side of the road was one time the property of Nathaniel Hickman. It has since been owned by John Hickman, Andrew J. Maloney, John Torbert and Robert J. Beswick. During Esquire Beswick's ownership he made vast improvements, both in buildings and the fertility of the soil. He said to the writer a short time before his death, that his farm paid a better income than any land he owned considering the amount invested. It originally contained but forty-two acres, but he added to it by purchase, until it now contains more than a hundred acres, although nearly one half is detached and is a short distance away. It is now the property of John B. Beswick, his nephew.

The next property is the farm of Mrs. Sarah H. Lister of Philadelphia, and is tenanted by Samuel C. Thomas. It is a large farm of perhaps three hundred acres and was formerly owned ny the late ex-Governor John W. Hall. Mr. Hall inherited about one half of this farm from his father and added to it by purchase the Fitzgerald farm of about one hundred acres and lastly he bought the Thomas Bowman tract of thirty-four acres which he also added. Governor Hall improved this farm very much in his time, but his daughter, Mrs. Lister, seems to have outdone her father in the matter of improvements. It is a valuable farm, conveniently located between two public roads as well as a cross road forming the western line. In the forties this farm was tenanted by George Bethards with a family of five children, all sons, who grew to manhood in this vicinity. William Henry, the oldest, learned the carpenters trade but finally abandoned it for the farm; George S. also learned that trade, at which he worked during his lifetime. he married and settled in Lebanon, where he died from injuries received by a fall from a building. John Wesley gave his life to his country in the great Civil War. James and Samuel are still living in Frederica, and William Henry lives in New Haven, Connecticut.

December 6, 1907

The next tenant on the farm of Mrs. Sarah H. Lister , partly described in our last article, was Mr. Jacob Quillen, then a young man who managed the farm for his widowed mother; assisted by two more brothers, Robert and Edward. Mr. Quillen still survives at the age of about eighty five years. The next was James Wyatt, with a family of five children - three sons and two daughters. Samuel, his oldest son, was a man of excellent traits of character who died in the prime of life. Joseph, the second son, was a spirited young man, with a disposition somewhat resembling a bundle of tow; quick to flas and soon to subside. Not withstanding this he was a man that loved his wife and children. He was killed in a railroad accident at Wyoming in 1867, leaving a wife and four children. George F. Wyatt the youngest son is a successful farmer in South Murderkill Hundred. Mary Ann married John Coverdale. They reared a family of six sons, most of whom are thrifty farmers. Susan married Samuel Coverdale and is still living. Job Coverdale followed Mr. Wyatt as a tenant, he had a family of nine children, five of whom are dead. He was a maternal grandfather of the present tenant, Samuel C. Thomas.

On this farm at the head of "Long Arm Branch," is an "iron ore bed" of considerable dimensions. As long ago as 1840, Mr. Peter F. Causey, then a leading business man of Milford and extensively engaged in the ore business, secured the right to develop it. He raised a large quantity, had it hauled to the landing on the farm now owned by Edward S. Beswick, and shipped a cargo to a smelting furnace at Egg Harbor, N.J. On testing it at the furnace it was found to be without value, and no more was shipped. The cause of its worthlessness was supposed to be on account of its proximity to the bay and ocean. It was a loss to Mr. Causey in a pecuniary point of view, but the large quantity of ore left on the landing and the pit from whence it was excavated, will remain as lasting monuments to his enterprise and business activity for generations to come.

Previous to the year 1842, there had been no public road from what was known as "Hall's Peach Orchard," to the "Big Stone" fishery. The traveling public was compelled to wind its way through pools of mud and ponds of water; many of the farms along this route were well nigh valueless on account of their inconvenient location. Some of these are now very valuable.

Living on the north side of this road and opposite Winlock Hall property was a large tract of land mostly in heavy timber, known as the "Tally Tract." It was bought about 1845 by G.S. and John W. Adkins, merchants of Milford, who associated with them in the purchase, Capt. William Thompson of Milford Neck. Captain Thompson was a prominent business man and a very influential citizen. He had formerly been a seafaring man, and had made considerable money in the employment of the government, carrying stone for the erection of the Delaware Breakwater.

They cut timber from the land, mostly into cord wood, which at that time was a staple commodity of trade from here to Philadelphia. After they had gotten off the timber they sold the land in three parcels; the first containing about one hundred acres, to William Fowler, who in turn sold it to James Slaughter. Slaughter sold it to John Wesley Hall. Mr. Hall has erected new buildings, planted extensive orchards and made of it a nice farm. It is now occupied by his son Bathuel W. Hall. The second parcel was sold to Warren Fowler, who built a small house upon it and lived there a few years after which he sold it to Thomas Lynch. After the death of Mr. Lynch it became the property of his son, T.J. Lynch, who occupied it for a while and sold it to John Wesley Hall; since which time it has been much improved. It is now occupied by his son William B. Hall. The third and last parcel was bought by Captain James Walton, and deeded it to his niece, Mrs. Catherine Evans, for a home. Mrs. Evans sold it in time of the rebellion to Mrs. Elizabeth Coverdale, the widow of Nathaniel

Coverdale, who bought it as an investment for her minor son, Joshua. When he reached his majority it took but a few years for him to get rid of the farm. It passed to the ownership of Paris T. Carlisle, who sold it to Alfred Hall, foster son of George Truitt - who also failed to keep it long. It again became the property of Mr. Carlisle who finally sold it to Thomas Mosely. Mr. Mosely has improved it, and by industry and thrift reaps good crops. He has the distinction of raising the largest strawberries that are grown in this locality.

December 13, 1907

The next farm to the Tally tract is now the property of Dr. F.L.Grier of Milford and tenanted by David Blizzard was for many years the home of Ezekiel Fitzgerald. He inherited it from his father and settled on it in early manhood. He had a family of six children - all sons. His oldest son, George Edward, was a bright boy, rather above the average for intelligence and managed to acquire a fair common school education, during his minor years. When grown he engaged in teaching and for several years followed that occupation. Finally he obtained a clerkship in a clothing store in Dover, Delaware, and later in Philadelphia. He was drafted during the Civil War but his patriotism quailed at the horrors of war and he "skipped" to Canada. The severity of the Canadian winter convinced him however that there is "no place like home," and he returned in the following spring. After the close of the war he married and went to Missouri, since which time he has been engaged in the Newspaper business in Kansas City.

In the last of the Sixties Ezekiel Fitzgerald sold his farm in Milford Neck and went to Sussex County, where he died a few years afterward. Three of his sons, David, Ezekiel and John, married and settled in Cedar Creek Hundred and have become thrifty farmers. Esquire James B. Davis bought the farm of Mr. Fitzgerald and improved it by erecting new buildings and repairing the old ones. After his death it went to his niece, Mrs. George S. Grier, and thence to the present owner. It is a level plateau of table land and well adapted to the growth of grass and grain and is susceptible of a high state of improvement.

The next place to be mentioned is a tract of land belonging to John C. Hall. It was one time the home of Ephriam Holliger, who lived there as long ago as 1840. he was a quaint individual of the genus homo, and lived almost as secluded as did Alexander Silkirk on the Island of Juan Fernandez, his home and farm being entirely surrounded by swamps and tall timber. He was a stout man and possessed of extraordinary lung power; his stentorian voice could be heard on a calm summer morning for miles away; his methods of farming were crude and primitive; his only team was a pair of large oxen, with which he plowed his ground, cultivated his crops and did his hauling; his twelve of fifteen acres of corn yielded him all to grain he needed; his pork was raised in the woods and fatted on the abundant mast of acorns this timber produced. Game was plentiful and he was quite a hunter using a flintlock musket of Revolutionary style, as a fowling-piece. He died about 1850, probably sixty years of age.

The next place is the property of George Macklin and consists of about four acres of land with a comfortable house upon it. This place was formerly a part of the land owned by Robert Scott, a colored man who lived near by at what is called Scotts Crossroads. Robert Scott, though covered with a black skin, was as pure and unsullied in character as any man; he was honest and upright, a devout and exemplary christian. No one feared to trust him knowing that whatever confidence they put in him would not be misplaced. He reared a family of twelve children, seven sons and five daughters all of whom he trained to habits of industry and sobriety and to respect the parental authority which was strict though not severe. In his home was the family alter from which daily he read a chapter from his bible and offered his earnest supplications from a soul filled with devotion. If not this, what is pure religion and undefiled before God and the Father? Robert Scott has long since gone to the land of the souls; the homestead has been torn away; the fields turned to a common, but the memory of him still lingers in the minds of those who knew him best. Fortunate would it be for his race if they would obey the precepts and follow the example of this pure minded man of simple life.

December 20, 1907

The small place below Scott's Crossroads is now owned by Mrs. Kate Sawyer of Camden, N.J., and occupied by her sister, Mrs. Mary Powell, and her Mother, Mrs. Elizabeth Jester. Mrs. Jester is the mother of twelve children, is ninety years of age, has her mental faculties unimpaired and her eyesight is sufficient to do needlework without glasses. She has a large fund of incidents and episodes of bygone days worthy of the attention of local historians. This property as long ago as the forties belonged to a colored man named Jordan Tindal. The tract then contained thirty-four acres. Tindal tried long and hard to sell it for the sum of one hundred dollars but failed to find a purchaser. About the last year 1856 it was sold to Masom D. Webb and Joshua Willey, who divided it into two parts, each building a house upon his half. Mr. Willey dying in a few years , it was held by his widow until her sons reached their majority, when it was sold to Reuben Cotterill, whose widow now holds it. Mr. Webb also dying in a few years his half sold to Col. C.S. Watson who finally sold it to Mrs. Sawyer.

The next farm is the property of Mark H. and James Willey and contains about one hundred and twenty-six acres. It formerly belonged to Winlock Hall who died in 1841. By virtue of his will it was left to his son, Draper Hall, during his lifetime, after which it descended to John A. Hall, his grandson, who was than a child. After John A. Hall arrived at age in 1857, he arranged with his father to get possession of the farm before his father's death. Including this farm John A. Hall had inherited about ten thousand dollars in real estate and money. But lacking habits of industry and sobriety and having little or no business training he scattered his fortune with a ruthless hand. In less than fifteen years he had so conducted his business that he was ready to retire for lack of funds to continue. He sold the remainder of his belongings in 1847 and went to Missouri where he died a few years later. The farm fell into the hands of John W. Stutzer of Milford. It was finally sold from him and bought by James Holland, grandfather of the present owners. By this time the title had become so twisted and tangled that it required all the legal acumen of the late Chancellor James L. Wolcott to unravel the kinks. James Holland was a man with traits of character strikingly peculiar; his disposition was gentle and lamb like except when aroused by insult of injury. He attended strictly to his own business and never meddled with the business of others. He and his brother Mark lived together for a lifetime and were never known to disagree. Two spinster sisters were his housekeepers. His older sister, Harriet, was married to James Dennis and was a model of industry and economy. Dennis, however, possessed no such redeeming trait. Individually he seemed to regard labor as the unpardonable sin and as persistently strove to shun it as if his soul's salvation had depended on such a course. He was of some use to the community however; he was an old line Whig of the Henry Clay type and an enthusiastic politician; he could discuss national affairs to the people of Milford Neck as earnestly, if not as intelligently, as Clay could in the Congress of the United States. He was several times elected as inspector of votes at the general election, but utterly failed to reach the exalted height of his ambition, which was to be Coroner of Kent County. Mr Dennis was an inveterate talker, a great wit and a man of considerable intelligence. He moved to Dover in the early fifties and died there a few years later. His only son, John Dennis, grew up a sober industrious young man and became a successful farmer.

The farm on the opposite side of the road now the property of Col. Robert H. Williams was for a long time the home of George Black who lived there many years. Mr. Black came from the Emerald Isle to this country when a young man; married and settled in Milford Neck. When the writer first knew him he had lost his first wife, his housekeeper being his oldest daughter, Mary Ann. He had three other daughters - Catherine, Sallie and Jane - all nearly grown. He also had a son - John - still a youth. Mary Ann married a Mr. Lee of Philadelphia, Catherine married a Mr. Walker also of that city, Sallie married Edward Mills, Jane died unmarried, John went to Philadelphia and located there. Toward the sunset of life, Mr. Black married Mary Hudson, daughter of the late Benjamin Hudson, and began to rear another family of children. By his last wife he had two children, George and Emma. About 1859 Mr. Black sold his farm to his son-ion-law, Edward Mills and located in Milford, where he spent the remainder of his life. Mr. Mills occupied the farm for a few years and sold it to William D. Webb, who in turn sold it to William L. Abbott. Mr. Abbott occupied it for a while and conveyed it to the late Reynear Williams, brother of the present owner. It was a very fine farm, nicely located and very productive. It is at present in tenure of Elias Macklin.

ISAAC R. JESTER

1908

COURTESY OF MILFORD CHRONICLE

44

January 3, 1908

The farm north of the Black homestead and adjoining it, was in 1840 the property of James T. Burley. It contained about one hundred and fifty acres, half of which was in heavy timber, a large percentage being white oak suitable for shipbuilding. The first man to occupy this farm as a tenant, within the recollection of the writer, was Robert Powell, an elderly gentleman with a family of five children and two brothers, William and Daniel G., who occasionally made their home with him. Mr. Powell was a sober, industrious farmer of the old school, and moderately successful. His home instead of being filled with the melodious strains of the modern parlor organ, resounded from morning till night with the hum of the spinning wheel and the clack-clack of the loom. Mrs. Powell and her daughter manufactured all the wearing apparel for her family, and the counterpanes, sheets, blankets, and table linen as well. The deft hands of all housewives of that day were alike employed in the same occupation; the belles and beaux of that day were almost universally clothed in homespun. Daniel G. Powell, brother of Robert Powell, deserves a special mention. He was a man from the common walks of life, possessing considerable ability for one of his time and opportunities, and had acquired a fair education. He was very industrious and usually worked as a farm hand during the farming season and taught school in the winter. Sometime in the early fifties he went to New Jersey to work and has not since been heard of by his friends and relatives here. He is gratefully remembered by a few elderly persons of today, who were his pupils more than half a century ago.

Captain Burley held the farm until his death, which occurred about 1854. It was then bought by James D. Sipple, who held it for more than twenty years and sold it to Peter L. Lofland the present owner. During all these years it has never been occupied by the owner, but has been "rented out" to tenants which in great measure accounts for its tardy improvement. While belonging to Captain Burley, it was rented on a long lease to a Jersey man named Francis Hamel, who occupied it solitary and alone for nearly two years, and then disappeared almost as mysteriously as he had come. He was eccentric almost to the point of dementia, and always carried an umbrella - no matter what the weather might be. His furniture was plain and scanty; his bed or berth in which he slept was suspended to the ceiling by means of cords and pulleys; by which he hoisted it up when he arose in the morning. He planted a peach orchard, but did not remain long enough to reap the fruit of his labor.

The farm adjoining this and extending beyond the road leading to Bennett's Pier, now the property of Dr. J.M. Luff of Felton, is one of the very best farms in this section. It has excellent buildings - all new and built of the very best material obtainable in this and the Philadelphia markets; built in the best workmanlike order and complete in every appointment. It was formerly the property of his father, the late N.P. Luff, who had a penchant for making his farms models of beauty. It is now tenanted by Sylvester D. Evans and his brother, John.

The next farm, on which Wilbur Mills resides, is also the property of Dr. Luff. As long ago as 1840 it belonged to the heirs of James Harrington and embraced the farm of Charles Macklin as one tract. But when the oldest son, John, became of age about 1847, he sold his share, being one-half, to James H. McColley. Mr. McColley also bought out the other heirs. He sold off the timber, a part of which was used for building the first jetty ever erected at the mouth of the Mispillion River for the improvement of the channel in 1850. Other of the timber was utilized in building the steamboat landing at Bennetts Pier, about one year later. This pier was a touching point for the steamer St. Nicholas plying between Philadelphia and Lewes, Delaware. Not a vestige of the pier or jetty exists today - except in the memory of the older inhabitants. After Mr. McColley had disposed of the timber, he sold that part lying south of the public road leading from the M.E. Church to Scott's Cross Roads, to Obediah Macklin, retaining that upon which the buildings were located. Toward the last of the fifties the remainder, which was sufficient to make a large farm, was sold to Richard Mills. After Mr. Mills death in 1888, it was bought by N.P. Luff. It now produces large crops of corn, wheat and tomatoes.

January 17, 1908

The next farm is a tract of about sixty-seven acres belonging to David S. Mills. It was one time the home of Manlove Cole, who owned and lived on it for nearly fifty years. Mr. Cole sold it to Luther Andrew, who turned it over to his son, John. Failing to lift the mortgage it became the property of Paris T. Carlisle. Mr. Carlisle sold it to David S. Mills, the present owner. Mr. Mills by his industry and economy has succeeded in paying for his farm and has improved his buildings and rendered them more comfortable and convenient. He has also make his land more productive. Not many men are better contented with their lot in life than Mr. Mills. He is a quiet unoffending man and one of Milford Neck's very best citizens.

The adjoining farm is the property of Charles Macklin. About fifty years ago this tract of worn out land was bought by Obediah Macklin, father of the present owner, at about five dollars per acre; at that time considered its full value. Mr Macklin was a very industrious man and immediately began to improve his new purchase by fencing, clearing and cultivation it. He had previously bought a small tract adjoining upon which he lived. Having land enough to make a snug farm he bent all his energies to accomplish that purpose. In 1859 he built a new and substantial dwelling on his new purchase and removed the buildings from the other to the same site. He was a careful cautious man and always conducted his business on a sound basis. Just as he was nearing the goal of his ambition, which was a comfortable home well provided, he was stricken with typhoid fever and died in the prime of his life, leaving a widow and six children. John M. Bennett married the widow and assisted in bring up the children occupying the farm until the death of his wife.

An interesting item connected with this property was the school house that stood near by on the same property. It was built in 1848, before Mr Macklin bought the land and was to take the place of the old church which had been used for that purpose and had outlived its usefulness. It was a wooden structure twenty feet square and one story high and stood corner-wise to the road. It had more the appearance of a small fort than an institution of learning. The first man to occupy it as a teacher was Rev. Charles P. Masden. He was a very excellent young man and a good teacher; he sickened and died before his term was completed. The winter term was taught by William H. Owens , a very pleasant teacher though not a profound scholar. Under his management of about sixty pupils, all youths and young men at that time, not more then ten are now living and these are well advanced in years. This Temple of Minerva remained on the same site until in the sixties the district was divided. Now came the tug of war; each half claimed the house. This contention grew more intense until Joseph Parsons, one of the committee of the original district, by advice of counsel, N.B. Smithers, removed the house from its former location to a central position in the old district. This ended the controversy and the newly formed district built a new house.

We all now notice the property of Eugene Voshell. It was formerly the property of the late Obediah Macklin, whose daughter married Mr Voshell. In the settlement of her father's estate this property fell to her and her older sister, Mrs. Joseph C. Bennett. Mrs. Bennett sold her interest to Mr Voshell who has since his purchase erected new and comfortable buildings and made it a pleasant home. He is a very industrious and thrifty young man and a carpenter by trade, whose services are always in demand. Nor is he alone to be complimented for his success in business; his wife is entitled to a full share of commendation.

The next place to be mentioned is situated north of the Voshell property. It is now owned by Daniel Scott, one of the sons of Robert Scott, a portrayal of whose life and character has already been given. Daniel Scott, though a colored man, has a reputation for veracity and integrity second to no man in this community of whatever race, color or nationality. He is in every essential a "son worthy of his sire."

This farm was for many years home of Joseph Jester, a staid old-time farmer with a large family. He was one of those easy going individuals who provided well enough for his family but never seemed in haste about anything. He lived within his means, paid his bills as he went and owed no man anything but goodwill. He died in 1858 aged about sixty years; leaving a widow and six children but one of whom was grown. His widow was a woman with more than average executive ability. She was a strict disciplinarian who managed to control her children so that they had a profound respect for her authority. Her oldest son, Joshua, about fifteen years old at his father's death, was a manly youth and with the assistance of his younger brothers, Albert and George, succeeded in managing the farm profitably and well. Their mother as a financier was hardly equaled in the community by any of her sex. She had the rare faculty of making the dollar go as far and accomplishing as much on its mission as any woman. She was a pattern of industry and economy and possessed more than an average amount of intelligence. She reared her children in such a manner that they have fulfilled the scriptural injunction by "rising up and calling her blessed." Joshua went to Iowa and became a prominent citizen there, having repeatedly been a member of the Legislature of that State. Albert went to Michigan and died there. George W. became a wagon builder and is now located in Wilmington, Delaware. The sisters, Mrs. David Coverdale and Mrs. Samuel French, also reside in Wilmington. Benjamin, an infant at the death of his father, is now the Rev. B. F. Jester, of Dover, Delaware.

January 31, 1908

Another family of Milford Neck which we have thus far failed to describe was that of William Thomas. Mr. Thomas was a man of considerable intelligence and well informed on general topics whose memory was remarkable and went back nearly to the beginning of the last century. He was a good conversationalist, clear in expression and could elucidate his subject in such a manner that is was plainly apparent to the comprehension of his listener. The writer distinctly remembers with what rapt attention, when a boy, he has listened to the conversation of this old gentleman. His home was situated near the M.E. Church, on a small tract of land now incorporated in the farm belonging to Joshua Bennett, Jr. It contained about twenty acres of land with a dwelling house of moderate dimensions.

His family consisted of a wife and three children, all boys. He was connected with the Thompson family by marriage, his wife being a sister of James Thompson. Mrs. Thomas was a very delicate constitution and was an invalid several years previous to her death.

William Thomas was somewhat peculiar individual. Although mentally brilliant he lacked those requisite qualifications necessary to success. He was honest and upright in his dealings with his fellow man but was never successful. He died in the centennial year, aged about seventy years.

Andrew T. Thomas, his oldest son, was a man of many parts He was in succession a farmer, a mechanic, a lecturer, a civil engineer, a school teacher, a sailor, a manufacturer, a postmaster, a merchant and finally an editor; all in a lifetime of sixty-eight years. He was a man of considerable erudition. In mathematics he was a veritable modern Archimedes; in composition he was a strong writer, a fairly good reasoner, but lacked continuity rather than general unsuccessful in his business ventures, though he always seemed to possess a good degree of perseverance. He married and settled on the old homestead which had become his property, and occupied it for a period of twenty-five years or more; reared a family of five sons, two of whom are mechanics, one a farmer and two who chose profession. Joseph is a minister of some note in the M.P. Church of the Virginia Conference, and has the distinction of being a brilliant pulpit orator. Walter worked his way through college and after graduating at Princeton adopted the study of law as his life work, and is now a rising young attorney of Philadelphia.

Andrew T. Thomas was the very first man in Milford Neck to espose the cause of the Republican Party. Himself, Dr. John S. Prettyman and James Brown cast the three votes for John C. Freemont for President in 1856 that were found in the ballot box at Milford. He died in nineteen hundred and one aged about sixty-eight years. His widow is still living.

William Thomas, his brother, was a plain young man of the practical sort, admired and respected by all that knew him. He was industrious and economical and ambitious to save the fruits of his labor. His career was cut short by death just as he had crossed the threshold of manhood. He died of measles of a malignant type in 1855, aged about 21 years.

Isaac M. Thomas, youngest son of the elder William Thomas, was considered a wayward youth but his faults were more the outcome of mischievousness than they were down right wickedness. When the Rebellion opened in 1861 he enlisted in the

First Delaware Cavalry and faithfully served his country during the war. He was in several hotly contested battles of the war, was captured by Stuart's Cavalry at Westminster and afterwards exchanged. When Grant took command of the Army of the Potomac, his regiment was dismounted and put in the trenches before Petersburg, but was soon restored to its former position. After the war was closed, Mr. Thomas, like Cincinnatus, again returned to his plow. He struggled on against adversity as best he could for several years, when in 1888 he bought the farm near Thompsonville now owned by John S. Reynolds. He occupied it for a few years and was getting on nicely when his mind gave way and his family was compelled to place him in an asylum. His son, Robert H. Thomas, a very industrious and worthy young man, conducted the farm until his mother's death in 1906, it was then sold. His children, six in number, are intelligent, useful citizens in the community and are comfortably in the affairs of life.

February 7, 1908

A short distance from Martin's Corner on the road leading to Milford, there is a farm of about 60 acres now the property of Thomas & Frazier of Frederica. It was for a long time the home of the late Benjamin P. Needles. Mr. Needles was a wheelwright and blacksmith by occupation and at one time did a thriving business. At first the dwelling house was not a very imposing structure, but after a few years of prosperity in his business, he was able to build a two story addition to the one he had formerly occupied. His family consisted of five members, himself, wife, wife's sister and two children of his wife's brother. Mr. Needles had his failings "as other mortals do" but he had redeeming traits; he contributed to the comfort of the "widow and fatherless." He was so devoted to the church that he might with very little injustice be called a religious bigot. His views were so narrow that he could scarcely tolerate any denomination but his own. His home was always open to the ministers of the church he attended.

His wife was a woman with a clear head and a kind heart. By her amiable disposition she had succeeded to a limited extend in rounding off some of the angles in her husband's austere disposition. Mr. Needles died about 1885 nearly eighty years of age. His widow survived him, dying in 1898 aged eighty-two years. These old people died childless and the property was bought by Mrs. Martha Harris, sister of Mr. Needles. Later it was bought by Thomas & Frazier who converted it into a truck and berry farm. It is nicely located in a progressive neighborhood and will soon be a desirable property.

The next place to be noticed is the home of Andrew J. Maloney, a retired farmer nearing the age of four score years. It was formerly the home of Daniel Mitten, for more than half a century. Mr. Mitten bought this property of Shadrach Postles in 1845 for a nominal sum and moved to it the following year. The improvements upon it being a single story one roomed house. Here he spent the one great effort of his life in building up a comfortable home. Here he reared his family of eight children with no other means of support except the labor wrought by his own hands. His home though humble, was a happy one for in this home he dwelt in the very bosom of his family; on this home the dove of peace descended and took up its abode. Mr. Mitten was a carpenter by trade and for a time the only one of importance in this vicinity. Little by little he added to his property in the way of improvements until he had a very comfortable as well as a happy home. Here he spent his early manhood; here he passed the meridian of his life and here he celebrated his golden anniversary. After his children were grown and had begun the battle of life for themselves, he sold out the homestead and removed to Frederica and died there in 1905 at the ripe age of 86 years. Mrs. Mitten though about 84 years of age is a well preserved lady and one whose lifework has been devoted to rendering her own home happy and contributing to the comfort and happiness of others. When the last lingering ray of the twilight of life will have faded away her memory will be treasured as sacred by those who survive her.

The farm situated on the north side of the road and opposite to the Needle and Mitten properties, was at one time the home of the late John Steward, and probably the birthplace of Ex-Postmaster John P. Steward. Mr. Steward occupied it as a home until about 1846; he removed to Milford. Renting his farm to Curtis Dilahay, a very industrious man of middle age with a large family of boys, who remained on it for several years. His force out-growing the size of the farm, he left it and moved to a larger one near Dover. One of his grandsons is now a salesman in the department store of George H. Hall. George Dennis followed Mr Dilahay as tenant and remained there until 1853 when Mr. Steward sold the farm to Joshua Torbert, a returned California gold-hunter. Mr. Torbert was a quaint specimen of humanity. Born on the Island of Malta in the Mediterranean Sea, by birth a Frenchman, by profession a seafaring man, by travel a citizen of the world. He came to his farm pretty well equipped with means but entirely destitute of practical experience. His theories were many and fine spun and his methods of farming were amusing to his neighbors but he was less a fool than a philosopher and profited by his mistakes until he had gained sufficient knowledge to conduct his business on a paying basis. One of the first things he did was to inaugurate a systematic and permanent improvement of his soil. He applied barnyard manure, lime and fertilizers, with a liberal hand and soon had a decided increase in the amount of his crops. In a few years he added about thirty acres more to his purchase and now had about one hundred acres of land. Mr. Torbert to occupied the farm for more than forty years when he rented it, bought property in Frederica and died there in 1901 well advanced in years. After his death the land was sold and Thomas A. Kirby became the owner. Mr. Kirby has erected a substantial and commodious dwelling, materially enlarged and improved the outbuildings, and farther increased the fertility of the soil. It is among the best in this locality and is in tenure of John W. Andrews.

February 28, 1908

The tract on the north of Thomas A. Kirby's farm and adjoining it was for a long time the home of Thomas Mason, a colored man. He was a carpenter by trade and had been an indentured apprentice to Daniel Mason, a prominent man and large land owner of Milford Hundred, from whom he took the name of Mason, it being customary in those days for the servant to take the name of his master. Thomas Mason was a remarkable man of his race. He was sober, industrious and very economical, by which he managed to secure a home and rear a large family. His farm contained about one hundred acres and was cultivated by his boys under his supervision, still he devoted the most of his time at work in his shop repairing wagons, building wooden harrows and cradling scythes for harvesting; these are now only relics of a former generation. He was a man respected by the white population and recognized as a leader by those of his color. He was the principal factor founding the A.M.E. Church known as John Wesley. This church had been named Mason's Chapel in perpetuation of his name. After his death in 1859, by virtue of his will the farm was divided into separate tracts and descended to three of his sons, while the fourth son received for his share a tract of about 40 acres which had been bought recently of James B. Anderson and was detached from the home farm. Of the estate of Thomas Mason one-half has passed out of the family. One of the four parcels is now the property of Dr. L.L. Carslile; the other the property of William Lindale. This property for late years has been considered hawked on the market; it had four owners P.T. Carisle, Alexander Mason, the Trust Company, Charles B. Witt and William Lindale.

The farm on the west side of the road was one time a part of the Lowery land, and as long ago as 1840 it belonged to Peter F. Causey, who at that time owned about one thousand acres in this section. Mr Causey in 1846 sold this tract to John Short for $750. It then embraced the farm of William E. Maloney and also part of the farm of Thomas A. Kirby and contained about two hundred acres. The first man to occupy this farm as a tenant, in the recollection of the writer, was James Salmons. Mr. Salmons was a very industrious man of a quiet disposition and very neighborly. He had a family of four children - three sons and a daughter - Thomas James, Robert Henry, Joseph and Sallie, all of whom grew up honored and respected citizens. Thomas James devoted his life work principally to farming, so long as he was capable of conducting that business, but for a number of years he has been sadly afflicted, having entirely lost his eyesight. Robert H. learned the carpenters trade, under the instruction of William G. Hering, became a good mechanic but sickened and died before he reached the zenith of his usefulness. Joseph grew up on the farm but later adopted railroading as his occupation.

Mr. Short took possession of the farm the first of 1847 and immediately began to improve it. He occupied it for a few years and buy the liberal use of Peruvian guano, raised large crops. About the year 1853 he bought the adjoining farm and moved to it. In the early sixties he sold the first purchase to Charles Warrington who occupied it for about four years and sold it to Daniel Burr of Cooperstown N.Y. for $7000. In a short time Mr. Burr sold about eighty acres to William E. and Russell B. Blore for $2000. The Blore brothers built on it and converted it into a fruit farm, but were not successful in their venture. Mr. Burr held the part on the west side of the road upon which the buildings are situated, containing about one hundred five acres until his death, which occurred in 1879.

Daniel Burr was a man of marked ability. Possessing a good education and a high moral character he was a good neighbor and a true friend; he was a devoted husband and an indulgent parent. His family consisted of a wife, two daughters and a son, all of whom were respected and esteemed. His son Daniel Burr Jr., went to the Pacific slope and located in Southern California. His younger daughter married Homer Lewis, a worthy young man formerly of Vermont, and now residing in Lincoln, Delaware. Miss Urania, the elder daughter, also resides in Lincoln.

A few years after the death of Mr. Burr the farm was sold to Dr. G.W. Marshall, who held it about fifteen years. In 1899 it was bought by George H. Jester, the present owner. Since his ownership he has improved it to such an extent that the land yields double the amount that it did when it came into his possession. He has also erected a new dwelling house of ample proportion, modern design and convenient arrangement, as well as a new horse barn and other outbuildings which add to the comfort and convenience of the farm. He now has a snug and cozy home, showing what energy and perseverance will accomplish. This farm has about sixty acres of cleared land and has more timber than any farm of its size in Milford Neck. It is nicely located with public roads converging from nearly all points.

March 13, 1908

The farm on the opposite side of the road is the tract sold by Daniel Burr, in 1870, to the Blore brothers. They held it about twelve years and sold it to Jered Alcott who held it until his death, which occurred in 1894. Mr. Alcott was a native of Northern New York, who came to Delaware in the last of the sixties. He was sharp, shrewd business man, viewed from a speculative standpoint and always on the alert as to the "almighty dollar." The farm we are now describing was in a fair state of cultivation when purchased by him, but under his management it deteriorated in value until when sold after his death it bought only about one-half the sum it had cost him. When purchased by William E. Maloney it was virtually without buildings. In 1894 when Mr. Maloney bought it he straightaway began to build upon it. He now has a comfortable dwelling with all necessary buildings required on a farm; all new and neat in appearance. Mr. Maloney is a practical mechanic as well as a neat and progressive farmer, and a very useful citizen in the community. He has a fair common school education, such as was obtainable in the public schools of thirty years ago. Added to this he has a large fund of good hard common sense and an indispensable commodity of success in the affairs of life. His home is cheerful and his farm is increasing in value as his crops increase in quantity.

The farm adjoining William E. Maloney on the east and containing about one hundred acres, now the property of Benjamin C. Needles and his brother, Theodore, has been in the Needles family for more that a century. According to records now in possession of the present owners, it was owned and occupied by their grandfather, John Needles, as far back as 1804. He was a blacksmith by trade and died on the farm in 1834. His widow, with her two children that were not grown, remained on the farm. Mrs. Mary Needles is remembered by the writer as far back as the early forties. She was a thorough going, energetic woman of nearly sixty years of age, having been born before the close of the Revolutionary War. Her recollection of events that transpired in the early history of the nation was vivid and trustworthy. She could discuss the incidents of the Mexican War in the late forties. She was possessed of a strong personality that served her well in her situation in life. The tough, wiry, mental fiber she possessed enabled her to manage her children, as well as her business affairs with more then ordinary ability. Her family at that time consisted of herself and two children - a son and a daughter - nearly grown. Her older children were married and gone to homes of their own. Her farm was poor and like every other farm in the neighborhood at that time yielded but small crops but she managed by her industry and perseverance, with the assistance of her children, to make a support. After her son, John P. Needles had reached his majority he married and settled near by. He cultivated the farm for his mother until her death in 1859, after which time he moved to it and took full control. John P. Needles was a man of rather more than ordinary ability for his time and opportunity. Naturally he was a man of rather more than ordinary ability for his time and opportunity. He was a mechanic and a man of resources; he could turn a hand to almost anything. He had an easy adaptation to the management of nearly all kinds of machinery, with which he came in contact. He was also an inventor; if he needed an article of machinery that had not yet been put on the market, he invented it and built it for himself. His disposition was always cheerful and bright; his spirit always buoyant as that of a boy; he enjoyed the sports - - especially that of hunting with all the enthusiasm of the youth. He seemed to concentrate his whole mind on whatever he undertook. His death occurred in 1875 of pneumonia at the age of about fifty years.

The Rev E.H. Miller in his funeral oration on the death of Mr. Needles, made the remark that "Milford Neck could not well afford to lose such men as John P. Needles," and he was right; the place made vacant in this community by his death has not yet been completely filled. His widow survived him about five years. Of the children there are six -- three sons and three daughters, all living; one in Oregon and one in Michigan, and one in New Jersey; while three -- two brothers and a sister -- occupy the homestead. Since their management of about 30 years, the farm has increased in value many fold. It now has buildings for any purpose a farm could require and located in such a manner as to resemble a small village, every building of which appears as fresh and neat as though they had been built yesterday and painted today. Benjamin C. Needles and his brother Theodore, have a model farm; they are up-to-date farmers and do their work neatly, almost to the very verge of fastidiousness.

March 20, 1908

On the south side of the Needles farm is located one of the farms of William G. Hering of Milford. It is situated between two branches of Fishing Creek, a small tributary of the Mispillion River. In physical structure it is an elevated plateau alternating between light and heavy surface soil underlaid with a heavy argillaceous sub-stratum and is as susceptible to a high state of improvement as any land in the vicinity. It is fortunately situated on account of having a natural drainage on both sides, an advantage not possessed by many farms. It contains about one hundred acres an ample portion of which is woodland. That part under cultivation grows abundant crops of all kinds of products indigenous to this climate. For twelve years past it has been under the management of Willard S. Voshell, who vacated it last January for a larger farm. Under his management the property in point of productiveness to its size became the banner farm of this neighborhood.

Mr. Hering is too well known to the present generation to need a very elaborate description of character by the writer. He is approaching the 80th parallel of life but is active for one of his age and his intellectual faculties are unimpaired. His youth and early life was spent in Milford Neck, but for more than fifty years his interests have been closely allied with the interests of the town of Milford and for most of the time a citizen of that place. He was appointed postmaster in Haye's administration and reappointed in the Garfield-Arthur administration, holding the office eight years.

Adjoining the farm of Mr. Hering on the west side is the farm of James H. Webb. It was for thirty-five years the home of the writer and embraced perhaps the most important period in the history of his eventful life. Here was met a few of the joys and many of the sorrows that fall to the lot of the ordinary mortal. Here the family chain was broken and here began the self sacrificing duty of caring for motherless children but the labor has not all together been in vain. Here life's darkest shadows fell but the clouds were not all gloom.

The property was formerly apart of the Lowery land and owned by Mr. Causey. It then had but a few acres of cleared land upon which stood a small single story house, occupied by tenants who were employed as day-laborers who usually shifted their quarters annually. The first of this class remember by the writer was Curtis Collins, who was a drinking man and when "in his cups" generally raised Cain in his family. He had two sons, Alexander and William, industrious youths who were usually hired to some farmer during the working season their wages being used to help support the family. They grew up to be respectable men and became prosperous farmers on their own account in after years. The next tenant was Mrs. Anna Wright, a widowed lady, and her grown up daughter, Sallie. They were poor but highly respected in the neighborhood and managed to make a comfortable living by the use of the spinning wheel and the loom. About 1850 it was bought by Sylvester E. Webb, of John Short. Mr. Webb built an additional one and a half story house to the one already there. This expenditure together with a large doctors bill compelled Mr. Webb to sell it to Dr. Thomas Cahall, a practicing physician of Frederica, who in short time sold it to Joseph French. Mr. French held it for a number of years during which time it was tenanted by his son, Nathaniel French, and later by Job Coverdale. Finally Mr. French sold it to Luther Andrew in 1867. One year later Mr. Andrew sold it to the writer who, after occupying it for 35 years and making vast improvements, sold it to James H. Webb, the present owner.

Prominent among the items of interest in this community which may be mentioned is the old school house No. 44, generally known as "Pine Grove Seminary." This literary institution has a history that dates back more than half a century. It was built in 1850, the building committee being Curtis B. Beswick, Shadrach Postles and Benjamin P. Needles, all of whom have long since passed away. Of the scholars that attended in the early fifties but a few remain and with them the tide of time is fast ebbing toward the sea of Eternity. Among those who were school fellows with the writer were Robert J. Beswick, William H. Bethards, George S. Bethards, Nicholas D. Hammond, Eli Adolphus Hammond, Thomas Humbrys, Samuel C. Herring, Kensey B. Jones, Tinley Postles, Theodore Sooy and Samuel Sooy, Jr., twelve in number all just merging into manhood. The destiny of these young men has been decided by inexorable logic of events. Several became farmers others mechanics and some tradesmen and business-men. As far as is known all were honored and respected citizens, thanks to the moral training they received. Of this number it is not known that more than five are now living. Others that have received the initial installments of their education in this school may be mentioned the names of Dr. Richard A. Marlim and later Dr. George Rhoads of Pennsylvania and Dr. John N. Rhoads and Dr. Samuel C. Meredith of the city of Philadelphia. Among the teachers that have been schooled there are the names of James M. Thomas, John C. Clifton, James A. Martin, S. May Beswick, Anna P. Beswick, Ida Mitten, Harry F. Mitten, Mary E. Martin, Lida Martin and George H. Jester. It has likewise produced two members of the Legislature, two members of the Levy Court, two trained nurses, two dentists and one attorney-at-law. Within the walls of this old school house there has been inculcated a code of morals that has gone far towards establishing the present status of society in this community. The morality of this section is not inferior to any other in the State. While the citizens may not have been as cultured as some other localities it is a noteworthy fact that but one homicide has occurred for more than seventy years.

April 3, 1908

The farm now the property of George S. Davis of Milford, and located on the road leading from Martin's Corner to Milford, was formerly a part of the Lowery homestead and belonged to Mr. Causey. It was then in one tract and had been separated from the adjoining farm which contained about 300 acres. About the year 1850 it was purchased by Shadrach Raughley, who shortly afterwards sold the part above mentioned containing about 150 acres to John W. C. Webb. Mr. Webb soon after sold about 60 acres to Thomas Lynch. At that time there was no building on it and Mr. Lynch began to build a dwelling house, pushing the work rapidly toward completion, when suddenly for some reason Mr. Webb refused to make a title to the property. The work on the house was suspended, a law suit for breach of contract ensued and Mr. Lynch was awarded cost of building and damages. Mr. Webb then sold his entire purchase including unfinished building to Robert B. Owens in 1855, who completed the house and moved into it. In about two years Mr. Owens sold it to James M. Jester, who in two years more sold it to Charles Mills so that in less than ten years it had five different owners. Mr. Mills, however, settled down to business and spent the remainder of his life on the farm. After his death in 1885 the farm was bought by George S. Davis who occupied it until 1903 when he relinquished farming and moved to Milford. Mr. Davis during his stay on the farm improved his buildings and increased the productiveness of the land more than five fold. He engaged in fruit culture in which he was very successful. He has an apple orchard of the finest fruit of this section. Mr. Davis is a thorough going whole soul man upright and persevering, a type of citizenship of which any community may well be proud. His farm at the present time is in tenure of Albert W. Short.

The farm on the opposite side of the road, the old homestead of the Lowery family, also belonged to Mr. Causey in the forties. After passing from him it became the property of John Short, who occupied it as a home for many years. In 1869 Mr. Short sold it to George H. Burhams of Poughkepsie, New York, for $6000. Mr Burhams remodeled the buildings, set out a peach orchard and made other improvements; flourished for awhile, ran short of means and finally sold out for less than cost to E.P. Potter and A.P. Lewis of Waterbury, Connecticut. These gentlemen took possession in 1872 and began operation as farmers. They were successful for a time, paying about $4000 on the purchase money. In 1877 Mr. Potter died leaving Mr. Lewis' family, keep up reprisals and pay interest on remainder of mortgage. The mortgage being foreclosed it was bought by John W. Hudson for about $3700. Mr. Hudson made considerable outlay in the way of improvements and finally became dissatisfied with his bargain and sold out at a sacrifice to Thomas A. Kirby. Since Mr. Kirby's ownership he has received enough in rents to reimburse him for the cost of purchase. It is now in tenure of William J. Trader, a first-class farmer.

Adjoining these farms is a plot of ground which time has rendered classic. This is the site where once stood that old memorable building the Baptist Church. Until within a few years ago there stood upon this hallowed spot an old wooden structure plain and unimposing, emblematic of the people who worshiped at its shrine. This old structure had resisted the relentless tooth of time for generations; so long that its history had been lost in obscurity. In all probability it was one of the first places of public worship erected in this vicinity and must have antedated the American

Revolution. It was substantially built and without ornamentation; its dimensions were about 20 to 26 feet and about 14 feet in height to the lower cornice; the roof reached its apex at an angle of about 45 degrees. Here in the early part of the 19th century the people of this neighborhood assembled to pay their vows and offer oblations to a Supreme Being. Nothing now remains to mark the location of the temple of worship except the mounds in the church yard where rests the ashes of the former worshipers of a half century ago.

April 17, 1908

Adjoining the school property, District No. 44, is the house of George Bennett, which he has occupied for about thirty-five years and reared a family of seven children, now all grown up. This tract contains about two acres. His occupation has been that of a carpenter but he has now nearly retired form the business.

Next to this property is the four acre tract late the property of John Wesley Hall but now belonging to a Mr. Raymond, formerly of Brooklyn, New York. This place in the early fifties as well as the property of Mr. Bennett was owned by Mr. Causey, who sold it to John Short. Mr. Short sold it to Collins Fisher, a colored man, who built a small house upon it and cleared the land. Fisher occupied it until his death, after which it was bought by John E. Wooters, a veteran of the Civil War, in 1870, who failed to pay for it. Subsequently it became the property of Daniel A. Thompson, who sold it to James H. Harrington a young mechanic. Mr. Harrington built a comfortable dwelling house upon it and occupied it as a home for several years. In 1901 he sold it to John Wesley Hall and moved to Milford. Mr. Hall occupied it about six years, sold out to Mr. Raymond and also located in Milford.

The farm situated east of Fishing Creek, on the road leading to Herings Corner, was one time a part of the Lowery land and also owned by Mr. Causey. About 1849 this tract was sold to a Mr. Stine in trust, for the heirs of John A. Brickel together with about forty acres of timber on the north side of the road. In 1847 John A. Bickel came from Pennsylvania to Delaware and with his wife located in Milford. His first business venture was to rent the Milford Mills belonging to Mr. Causey and engaged in the milling business. He was not very successful in the undertaking and abandoned it in two years, his father-in-law having bought the farm of Mr. Causey - - Mr. Bickel moved to it and began farming. The land was poor, the buildings were dilapidated and Mr. Bickel inexperienced as a farmer. But he was a strong athletic young man of German descent and struggled on against opposing conditions with slight success, until he had raised a peach orchard. After his orchard came into bearing and proven remunerative he further embarked in the berry culture, which proved very profitable. Mr. Bickel erected new buildings improved his land and laid up money. He reared his family of six children on the farm which had at the time of his death increased in value ten fold. John A. Bickel was a good citizen, a man of considerable culture and was greatly respected in the community. He died in 1905 aged about 84 years. His brother William P. Bickel, was the first artist to take a daguerreotype in the town of Milford, and in about twelve years after the discover of the process by Louis Dagnarre, the French scene painter of Paris.

During the life time of John A. Bickel this tract of land was divided into two farms, one of which is now the property of his oldest son, William H. Bickel; the other the property of his second son, Samuel E. Bickel. William H. Bickel is a thriving, prosperous farmer, in spite of the fat that he has grown more tomatoes for defaulting canners than any other man in Milford Neck. It seems remarkable that he has been caught in the swirl of every collapsing firm in the business, but he has been very successful with his crops of peaches, nearly always realizing fair prices and receiving prompt returns. He is a jolly good natured man and so cheerful in disposition that he can laugh at his own calamities.

Samuel E. Bickel owns the other farm, where his father lived for more than fifty years of his life-time. It is valuable as a grain and fruit producing farm. It is nicely located in a thriving neighborhood and is in a high state of cultivation. The buildings are comparatively new and conveniently arranged. It is one of the most desirable properties in this locality.

April 24, 1908

Samuel E. Bickel, who owns the farm last described, also owns and occupies another adjoining it containing about 67 acres. This farm and the one adjoining was formerly owned by Collins Stevens, an elderly man who came form Maryland and bought it about 1846, of whom the writer is not prepared to say. Mr. Stevens had two grown up sons -- William Henry and Thomas. Mr. Stevens died a short time after buying this farm, and it was divided between his sons; Thomas Stevens received as part of the tract that which now belongs to Samuel E. Bickel. This was sold to the late David Collins, for many years a merchant of Milford. At that time it was mostly in timber, and when Mr. Collins had gotten off the timber, he sold the land to Soloman Hevelow a colored man, who built a small house upon it and cleared a part of the land. Failing to pay for it, it was sold, and Harry C. Corsa became the owner, in the last of the sixties. Mr. Corsa occupied it for several years as a home, and sold it to Samuel E. Beckel. Since Mr. Bickel has owned it, he has improved it by erecting a new and substantial dwelling house, barn and other buildings. He has also very much improved the fertility of the soil. It is well supplied with fruit of various kinds and is a very desirable home.

That part of the original tract which fell to the ownership of William H. Stevens, is now the property of William B. Hering. William H. Stevens was a sailor by profession and a man of considerable ability. He was captain of a vessel plying between Frederica and Philadelphia, for several years, finally he quit the water and engaged in store keeping at Fork Landing. He sold his farm to Captain John Taylor in 1855, who occupied it for several years, when misfortune overtook him in the loss of his wife. He was left with a number of small children, and under the severe strain he could not meet the conditions of his obligation. The mortgage was foreclosed and he and his motherless children were rendered homeless. It was next bought by a Mr. Andre, a shoemaker by trade, who came from Maryland. Mr. Andre died in a short time, leaving a widow and four children; she struggled against adversity and succeeded in bringing up her children, after a fashion. At her death the property was purchased by Robert J. Beswick, who improved it and made it a very desirable place, by erecting new buildings and adding to the fertility of the land. After his death it descended by bequest to his nephew, William B. Hering, who now occupies it.

William H. Stevens after selling his farm, also sold his store at Fork Landing, to a John A. Hall of Milford Neck, and located in Burrsville, Maryland, where he accumulated quite a large estate. His wife was a daughter of the late Abraham Todd and a sister to the young man who met his tragic death by perishing in the terrible snow-storm of February 22nd, 1857, near McColley Mills.

The farm situated on the south side of Fishing Creek, and on the east side of the road leading to Milford, now the property of Lavinus Austin, and containing about 70 acres, was formerly a part of the tract now belong to the heirs of S. Todd Jenkins. It was bought in 1883 by Abraham Austin, father of the present owner. Mr. Austin, with his family, moved into it in May of that year. His family consisted of himself, wife, three sons and a daughter-in-law. Mr. Austin's oldest son, William, died the following year; about 32 years of age. Mrs. Austin died in 1889, aged 67 years; her husband survived her until 1891, when his death occurred at the age of 76 years. Lavinus Austin, who previously to the death of his parents, had been at the head and front of affairs, now became sole proprietor. He has erected a large and commodious dwelling house, of modern style and finish, and other buildings suitable and convenient for farm purposes. When he first came to Delaware, like many others, he was for awhile dissatisfied, but having an easy adaptation to surrounding circumstances, he gradually became contented. He embarked in fruit culture, and in that industry succeeded very well, he also entered the political arena, and as a result, was rewarded by being elected a member of the Legislature. He is a man of considerable information and a good conversationalist, and by his residence of 25 years has apparently became a native Delawarean. His wife is a lady of culture, and possess those traits of character, of rendering her home cheerful and happy; for which her sex in the Northern States are proverbial. Their home at the present time has but three members -- Mr. Austin, his wife, and one youthful son; their older son being employed as bookkeeper in a Bank in New York City. Frank F. Austin, brother of Mr. Austin, and well and favorably known in this vicinity, is a citizen of Woodbridge, New Jersey.

May 1, 1908

The next farm described is the farm of the late Silas T. Jenkins. This place, in the early forties, was the property of Captain William Thompson and contained about three hundred acres. At that period of time it was one of the most productive farms in this section the entire tract embraced the 70 acre farm of Lavinus Austin and also the 40 acre tract of Dr. J.M. Rhoads. Captain Thompson was a man of great business energy and a very successful farmer. He had acquired quite a snug estate as a sailor in previous years, by carrying stone for the construction of the Delaware Breakwater. He was a popular man and a very influential citizen, a politician of the Jackson school of Democracy and though often nominated for office, never elected, on account of his party being hopelessly in the minority in this State. About the year 1851, Captain Thompson sold his farm to Samuel Sooy of New Jersey, and moved to a dairy farm near an elderly gentleman, with several grown up sons. He occupied the farm about four years during which time he raised immense crops, especially corn. Some years he grew as much as two thousand bushels. This was when the farming industry was being revolutionized by the use of Peruvian guano. Mr. Sooy made considerable improvement , divided it into two farms; finally he sold it to Col. H.B. Fiddeman, a wealthy business man of Milford. Colonel Fiddeman owned the property about ten years and sold it to Silas Todd Jenkins, a Pennsylvanian, in 1865. About this time the planting of peach trees had become as craze in this peninsula and Mr. Jenkins like many others caught the infection. It was a desperate attack and lasted until he had nearly 100 acres in trees. When they came into bearing he not only had more than he could handle profitably, but more than he could save in any condition. During the early seventies, when the peach culture was at a discount he failed to realize enough in many instances, to pay the cost of transportation. Later on he erected an evaporating plant and in a financial point of view, was a little more successful.

Silas Todd Jenkins was a man whose life and character was strickingly peculiar. He was not one of those individuals with whom a stranger would be favorably impressed and yet his character was as grand and sublime as the granite hills that surrounded his former Pennsylvania home. An acquaintance with Mr. Jenkins of nearly thirty years as a neighbor led the writer to believe that he was a man without guile. His religious views inclined to the Society of Friends, but he usually attended the Baptist Church; his wife being a member of that society. He contributed liberally to the maintenance of that church. He was one time elected to the Levy Court of Kent County and faithfully and honestly discharged his duties to his constituents, but was unpopular with many of his fellow members, because of his pronounced opposition to schemes of graft and speculation.

Mr. Jenkins was a man of progressive ideas and great industry and gave much employment to the working classes of this section. He was interested in the good Roads Program and did everything he could for the traveling public, in opening and building new roads. After encountering decided opposition he succeeded in getting a public road from the Old Baptist Church to the Tub Mill, which is now conceded to be a public benefaction. His purchase of the Tub Mill, can scarcely be regarded as a financial success; it increased his responsibilities and added but little to his income. For general information Silas T. Jenkins was well booked up. In literature, science and the arts, he was quite proficient, but in business matters he was not what the worldly minded recognizes as a success. He died in 1989 about 74 years of age, honored and respected most by those who know him best. His widow is still living and is quite active for one of her age.

May 8, 1908

The farm now owned and occupied by John W. Short, was once the homestead of Shadrach Postles. How long it was in possession of the Postles family the writer is not prepared to say. Back in the forties he lived there and had perhaps for many years. He had raised a family of six children several of whom were grown. Mr. Postles was an old time gentleman and represented that type of citizen contemporary with the first half of the nineteenth century. He was somewhat prominent in business affairs in his neighborhood and took a great interest in the Free Schools which in his time were only beginning to develop. His children received a liberal education for the time-one of the them the eldest son-becoming a skillful surveyor. In politics he was an Old Line Whig and in 1846 was elected by that party to the Levy Court, in Kent County, which position he held four years. Mr. Postles died in 1857, probably something more than three score years of age. The farm was sold by the administrator for the closing of his estate and was bought by the second son, Zadoc Postles, for the sum of three thousand and fifty dollars. Zadoc Postles, owing to the financial crisis following the Walker Tarrif tinkering of Buchanans administration was compelled to sell it 1860 at a small sacrifice. It was bought by John Short, who owned the adjoining farm, and whose ready money relieved Mr. Postles of his financial embarrassment. It should be remembered that during almost the entire administration of Mr. Buchanan the country was passing through monetary crisis. Wages were low and business was depressed, but the currency of the country was sound and those having money knew its value as a purchasing power. Mr. Short paid three thousand dollars for the farm but owing to the event of the Civil War and the inflation of the currency, in less than five years it had increased in value more than one hundred per cent. Soon after he purchased the farm he rented his other and moved to it. His first wife died soon after this and his six children being grown he married again and began the raising of another family. Mr. Short died in 1894, probably 80 years of age, leaving a widow and her seven children the result of the second marriage. Mr. Short was a shrewd business man and had accumulated most of his means by speculation in the land. His oldest son, by his second wife, now owns the farm. It is a fine farm of about one hundred acres. Since his ownership he has made great improvements both in buildings and fertility of the soil. Recently he has erected a large stock barn which is second to none in this section. He has installed in it a gasoline engine which furnishes power for the cutting of food and grinding of grain for all of his stock and poultry. He grows large crops of grain and is very successful in fruit culture.

Adjoining this is a farm of 83 acres formerly a part of the same tract and owned by Shadrach Postles. After his death it became the property of Listen A. Houston and occupied by him for several years. He sold it after the close of the war in 1865 to Mrs. Harriet Jackson of Wilmington, Delaware, who with her family occupied it for several years more and then sold it to Harry Linderman, a blacksmith from property of William E. Kelley who occupied it for fourteen years and in 1907 sold it to Frederick T. Sharp. All these years there has been no improvements made upon it until purchased by Mr. Sharp who has already erected a large stock and hay barn. The industry and perseverance of which he and his wife possessed will most likely redeem it from its former neglected condition and make it compare favorably with the adjoining farms in this section. They are young people coming from families of industry, economy and thrift and eventually will be certain to succeed.

May 29, 1908

Adjoining the farm of John W. Short and located west of it is the farm of George T. Hill, now of Milford. It is a fine farm in a high state of cultivation, and has for many years been considered one among the best in this vicinity. It was formerly the property of James Postles and embraced the land lying on the south side of the road, now owned by Charles Postles. The entire tract before being divided contained more than two hundred acres. Prior to the middle of the last century it was considered one of the best managed farms in this section. From the earliest recollection of the writer until 1855 it was occupied by Mr. Postles himself, who was a farmer in the strictest sense of the term. He was one of the pioneers in the renovation of worn out land in this part of Kent county. In the early forties, the farming business was at a low ebb. About this time the business of the country was at a standstill and none more so than farming. Commercial manures were unknown except lime and even that was a doubtful experiment. Mr. Postles early imbibed the spirit of improvement and was the first farmer in this section to introduce the growing of clover, by which means he made it possible to introduce improved methods of threshing grain. He was the first man in this vicinity to purchase and introduce a horsepower and threshing machine. Previous to this time it had been the custom of farmers to tread out the grain with cattle or horses, or to use a pair of horses hitched to a machine, with the name of tumbling-tom. It was simply a log of wood about seven feet long and ten inches in diameter with rows of strong pegs inserted three inches apart around he entire circumference, and cut to a length of about eight inches. Who was the inventor of this machine is not known, but it was thought to be a very great improvement over threshing by hand, with the old time implement called a flail. The machine of eight horse power had a capacity to thresh about three hundred bushels per day, but it was very seldom that quantity was found on one farm. Many of the farms that now yield a thousand bushels a year did not yield one hundred at that time. With the aid of clover, lime and Peruvian guano Mr. Postles' farm soon became one of the most productive in this part of the county.

About the year 1855 Mr. Postles built a large dwelling house, barn and other necessary buildings on an adjoining tract fronting the State road. This land was mostly in timber of worn out land that had not been in cultivation for a number of years and grown up in pine and cedar. By virtue of much hard labor, and with an outlay of considerable money he succeeded in a few years in making it, not only one of the most handsome but one of the best paying farms in this section. This farm is now the property of Dr. James G. Stanton and is regarded as one of the most beautiful places on the road leading from Milford to Dover. Shortly after the Civil War he bought another farm. It is situated on the "Lowber Farm." After the purchase of this farm he erected new buildings and improved it so that it produced a large revenue. It now belongs to the heirs of the late John W. Kirby.

James Postles was a man whose disposition was stern and inflexible. When his course was fully determined and his purpose fully decided upon, they were well-neigh as invincible as the laws of Medes and Persians, but when his sympathies were enlisted in behalf of the needy and deserving he was a true friend. He was a strictly conscientious man, and his religious principals consisted largely of conforming to the test of scripture in the Gospel of St. James: "That ye visit the widow and the fatherless in their affliction and keep your self unspotted from the world."

His wife, familiarly known as "Aunt Betsy" was a kind hearted lady and more like a mother than aunt to most persons. No writer of modern times has in as few words more fittingly described the character of Aunt Betsy Postles than Alfred Tennyson when he wrote:

"Kind words are more than coronets,
And simple faith than Norman blood."

Though without children of their own, she and her husband raised a family of fourteen , one of which was but nine days old when she was placed under their care and protection. This was Sarah Elizabeth Postles a niece of Mr. Postles and when grown became the wife of the late James H. Bell. Of the fourteen children reared by them the only one born under their parental roof was Col. Theodore Townsend, a grand-nephew of Mrs. Postles, who spent the greater portion of his minor years in their home.

Aunt Betsy Postles was a diplomat. She had an influence over her husband that no one else ever possessed. Figuratively speaking she could wind him around her finger; a performance no one else would dare attempt.

In the early part of 1861, when the dark clouds of disunion hung like a pall over the nation, and men were dazed and undecided what course to take, James Postles was one of the first men in this section, to plant himself squarely and unalterably in defense of the Union. From his family went out several members to fight in its defense. After the close of the Civil War Mr. Postles retired from the farm, bought a property in Milford and resided there until his death. He died in 1882 after an active life of seventy-six years. Mrs. Postles survived her husband nearly ten years, having lived to the ripe age of eighty-four years. Mr. Postles left an estate of about thirty-thousand dollars. Not many men and women have wielded a greater influence or stamped a deeper impress upon the community in which they lived than this honored and respected pair, whose worthy example succeeding generations can well afford to emulate.

June 12, 1908

On the south side of Postels homestead is a tract of land of about one hundred acres or more extending from the southern arm of Fishing Creek to the State road. This was one time the property of Joseph Houston, a colored man, who for many years occupied it as his home. It is one of the most desirable pieces of farm land in this section. Joseph Houston was a man of more than average ability for his race. He held a prominent place among the farmers of his day, and was largely influenced by his friend and neighbor, James Postles, whose example he persistently tried to imitate. He was one of the few men of his race whose progressive operations in the farming business resembled those of the Caucasian race. He improved his land, attended strictly to his business and was with all a law-biding and order-loving citizen. He died in 1861 probably 70 years of age. By virtue of his will, he left his estate to his son-in-law Caleb Bell, in trust for his grandchildren, with the provision that Caleb should build a school house in a suitable place, on the farm, for the education of colored children. This obligation Bell faithfully performed, but it involved him financially for life. The institution seemed to prosper for a while, but after a few years it went into decline and finally collapsed for lack of proper support, and Houston's life-dream became a failure. The building has long ago been removed and but little now remains to mark the spot where it formerly stood. That part of the farm has become the property of Dr. James G. Stanton who has attached it to his farm. Only about two-thirds of the original tract is now in possession of the heirs of Joseph Houston. A strange fatality seems to follow the accumulation of wealth by colored men of this section.

We now come to notice the farm adjoining, which is one of the farms belonging to the Potter Estate. This estate is supposed to be owned by the poor of Kent County, outside of the Poor House, but the greatest beneficiaries of this charity, have been those who would resent the slightest intimation that they belonged to that class.

In order to make it apparent to the minds of the number of readers, it will be necessary to go back to the time of Col. Potter's death, in 1843. Col. Benjamin Potter was without doubt the wealthiest man in Milford hundred, perhaps in Kent County, in his day and generation. By his will he bequeathed to the poor of Kent County, outside of the Poor House, a large number of farms besides other property for the purpose of establishing a perpetual fund for the benefit of the unfortunate class. Of course so large an estate could not be managed without a trustee, and directly after the will was probated, Chancellor Johns appointed Charles T. Fleming to that position.

Much of the property at that time was in bad condition and almost entirely failed to produce any revenue. Several of the farms were occupied by tenants who refused to pay any rent, so that what little was left after the Trustee's salary was paid, was spent in litigation. In a few years the condition of the farms became so deplorable that they failed to be self-sustaining, much less affording any income for the benefit of the poor. In 1859 Chancellor Samuel M. Harrington issued a decree, that a part of the property should be sold and the proceeds applied to the improvement of the others. This action of the Chancellor wrought a great change in the appearance and in the utility of this property.

The years 1860 was a busy one for Mr. Fleming, the trustee, as well as for the mechanics he employed. New and comfortable dwelling houses and ample barns were erected on several of the farms; on others the buildings were put in good repair and rendered comfortable. After this a new system of leasing was adopted by Mr. Fleming which he called an improvement lease and was to run for twenty years.

In the year 1867 an effort was made by W.N.W. Dorsey, Esq., to oust Mr. Fleming from his position as trustee, but it failed to materialize. Hon. Daniel M. Bates then being Chancellor, was not the man to be influenced by partisan prejudice and the attempt proved abortive and Mr. Fleming continued trustee until his death, a period of about thirty-eight years. During this time a sum equalled to about nine thousand dollars had accumulated in the fund for the poor of Kent County from the proceeds of the estate. Although for many years this "knotty" question had been wrestled with, by prominent members of the bar, it had not yet been decided who were the proper ones to receive this charity. But now they went to work with a determination to do something -- and they did-they succeeded in the distribution of the entire surplus without any apparent benefit to anyone, except the legal profession. They also decided that the estate must be sold at public auction, and in conformity it was extensively advertised to be sold at Milford, in June 1881, at which time and place the Chancellor attended with his legal advisors, auctioneer, a clerk, etc. The sale actually commenced at the appointed hour when the Hon. N.B. Smithers discovered suddenly that it could not be legally sold. The sale was called off without further ceremony, and thus ended the greatest farce in the Potter Estate. Chancellor Saulsbury appointed John Harrington, to succeed Mr. Fleming, and a different system of management was inaugurated which seemed to be an improvement over the former method. Under Mr. Harrington's management the property seemed to increase steadily in value.

June 26, 1908

In continuation of our brief sketch of the Potter Estate we would mention the fact that Chancellor James L. Walcott was the first to decide who were the recipients of the fund derived from this estate. He decreed that the proceeds should be at the disposal of the trustees of the poor, to dispense to those who by an allowance of a small sum per month could manage to live without becoming an inmate of the Almshouse. Since his decision this method of distribution has been steadily followed and seems to give very general satisfaction. After the death of Mr. Harrington, in 1900, Hon. John W. Causey was appointed his successor by Chancellor John R. Nicholson. Mr. Causey takes a deep interest in the property, and under his supervision it has been still further improved. These are splendid farms and well deserve the care and attention Mr. Causey bestows upon them. The particular farm which we are now describing is in tenure of Charles Parker Taylor, an up-to-date farmer and a hustler. Though not to the "manor born" he is in nearly every essential a typical Delawarean. He is industrious, persevering and economical almost to a fault. He has reared a family of six children, all of whom reflect great credit upon their parents. Two of his daughters are teachers in the Public Schools. His only son, Charles Edwin, is a young man of excellent traits of character; sober, industrious and persevering and will undoubtedly fill the role of valuable citizenship. Mr. Taylor deserves much credit for the manner in which he has succeeded in life. For a quarter of a century Mr. Taylor has lived on land of the Potter Estate during which time he has worked hard and accumulated a competency.

On the south side of the road leading from the State road to the old Baptist Church, is a tract of land now divided into two farms and containing about 270 acres which formerly belonged to Moulten Cropper, maternal grandfather of Col. Theodore Townsend. Mr. Cropper died in the last of the forties and the land was sold to close his estate, and was bought by Eli F. Hammond, James H. Hammond, and Mrs. Thomas Virden.

At the time of Mr. Hammond's purchase the land was not very productive, but by the use of guano, which was well adapted to the restoration of worn out land, he made good crops and realized snug profits in growing grain. The use of Peruvian guano wrought a complete revolution in the farming industry of this section. Farms that had previously grown from one to two hundred bushels of wheat were now made to yield six or eight hundred bushels and prices were very remunerative. In the decade of the fifties the ruling price of wheat ranged from $1.25 to $1.50 per bushel, and later during the War it reached the enormous price of $3.05 per bushel. Men of wheat producing land like Mr. Hammond bought the property which he divided into two farms of about a hundred and thirty five acres. After his death the property was sold for the distribution of his estate. One of these now belongs to Charles Davis; the other to George H. Davis, his brother. These farms are located in an agricultural community that is inferior to none in Kent County. The owners are energetic men and practical farmers and under their care these farms are destined to reach a high state of fertility.

Adjoining these farms and to the east of them is another, now the property of George H. Davis. It one time belonged to Charles T. Fleming and was known as the New Design tract. Since it has been the property of Mr. Davis he has erected new buildings upon it and cleared up the land so that he not only has a pleasant home but a profitable farm also. In the development of this place, in the few years he has owned it, Mr. Davis has shown what vim and energy will accomplish when properly directed. Mr. Davis comes of a long line of industrious ancestors, and has faithfully maintained the standard, per excellence. He is still comparatively a young man and has not yet relaxed his former ambition. His example shows emphatically the possibilities of any young man in this section, if he be possessed of a clear head and stout heart.

July 3, 1908

We will now describe the farm, for many years the property of the late Charles T. Fleming of Milford. It is nicely located on the northern side of the Mispillion River, and south of Fishing Creek, a tributary of that stream, and contains about two hundred acres.

In the more ambitious portion of Mr. Flemings' life, this farm was to his fancy, a veritable Utopia; upon it he set his highest standard of value. He was a man of lofty ideas, and his prescience enabled him to discern through the vista of the future, the wonderful possibilities it contained. Mr. Fleming's time, however, was too nearly absorbed with other duties to bestow proper care and attention to farming, or even upon his farms-hence they were often neglected. But this farm was his special "hobby." He was a surveyor, draughtsman, conveyancer and notary public, for more than forty years and probably during his life acknowledged more deeds than any other man that ever lived in Milford. He was also a man of considerable literary ability. After the first newspaper was issued in Milford, September 30, 1848, he became a regular contributor, both in prose and in verse. His conception was accurate, his style conforming to that of the early half of the Nineteenth Century. His life was so long and useful, the major portion of which was spent in Milford. Mr. Fleming died childless leaving his estate in fee simple, to his wife who was the sister of the late James S. Richards. Mrs. Fleming survived her husband several years.

The first tenant remembered by the writer, to occupy this farm was John Wilkerson, who wife was a niece of Mr. Fleming, and a sister of the late Joseph Haslet Owens, Mr. and Mrs. Wilkerson were the parents of Samuel O. Wilkerson, a wealthy and respected citizen of Milford.

At the time, Mr. Wilkerson lived on this farm it was quite productive for that period, but not as high a state of cultivation as at the present time; the science of farming was not then so extensively developed, as it is now. Although Mr. Wilkerson was a man of much energy and push, and was regarded as one of the best farmers of his day, it is doubtful if he grew yearly more than one hundred bushels of wheat on the farm, especially before introduction of guano. Corn and oats were the principle cereals grown at the time.

There was a large apple orchard on the farm, consisting mostly of winter apples, such as russets, winesap and Winter Grizone, and it would be surprising to the present generation, to see what crops were gathered, they were simply immense. They were gathered in the fall and hauled by cart loads, to be hurled in pits in the ground for winter use. Children were not then lavishly supplied with modern candy and poisonous confections, but had plenty of ripe wholesome fruit for Christmas and other extra occasions.

Apart from the poverty stricken condition of the soil, farmers had much less to contend with then than now; Colorado beetles, San Jose scale, cuculio and peach yellows were unknown.

Next after Mr. Wilkinson, as a tenant, was Jacob Quillen, then comparatively a young man, now still living at the ripe age of about eighty-five years, one of the very few of that time who still survives. Following Mr. Quillen came Hezekiah Masten, a young man who began farming on this place, but after a few years bought the Charles Fleetwood farm, near Mordington Mills and occupied it for many years. Mr. Masten died in Milford a few years ago about seventy-four years of age. In the early seventies Dickerson M. Meredith became the tenant. During his occupancy, Mr. Fleming erected new buildings on the farm and made other improvements. After the death of Mrs. Fleming, widow of Mr. Fleming, this farm became the property of Mrs. Samuel W. Kinder, by inheritance, since which time Mr. Kinder has bounteously bestowed improvements upon the farm, in such a manner that the Utopian dream of its former owner seems almost certain of realization. This farm is without a doubt one of the finest of the many fine farms located along the river. When seen by the writer it presented a beautiful picture-a picture on which the land is sufficiently undulating to afford a very picturesque appearance and render the landscape exceedingly beautiful. Away in the distance stand clumps of forest trees -- oak and pine -- whose giant branches, clothed in Nature's livery, stand out in bold relief against the horizon. In addition to those natural beauties, the farm is systematically arranged into four fields, of about twenty-four acres each, besides ten acres in fruit trees consisting of apples, pears, cherries, etc. There is also another ten acres or more in peach trees, two years after setting, which are more promising in healthfulness, and more beautiful in symmetry than any thing this writer has seen for a long time. Two fields were in wheat, one planted to corn, and last but not least, the fourth, well set in clover. The buildings were comparatively new, conveniently arranged, and had been recently painted. The farm work was kept well in hand by Mr. Walls, the tenant, who seems to take as much pride in the management of the farm, as Mr. Kinder does in furnishing the improvements. Evidently this is the true relationship between tenant and landlord. If all tenants were as neat, reliable and trustworthy, as William B. Walls, landlords would have much less reason to complain.

July 31, 1908

The property lying to the north of the last farm described, and immediately on the road leading to Milford, and known as the "Burnt House" tract, has a history that is not altogether interesting. In order to give a few of the salient features of its history, the writer will be compelled to anti-date his own personal recollection, by stating a few facts which are echoes of a former generation. According to reliable information, there stood upon this farm a brick house, which was occupied by Robert Powell, as a tenant, as long ago as 1830. A daughter of his, and an aunt to the writer by affinity, now more than ninety years of age, was a girl at the time of about twelve or fourteen years. The vivid description she so graphically portrays, of the burning of that building, appeals with much interest to the mind of the listener.

On a cold frosty morning in mid-winter, the ground being covered with snow to the depth of about eight inches, and while the family was at breakfast, it was discovered that the house was on fire. A hasty investigation disclosed the fact that the roof was all a-flame and nearly ready to fall in. Little time was afforded to save any property; barely time to escape. The family consisting of husband, wife and children, houseless and homeless, started on their disconsolate march to the nearest neighbor, nearly a mile away on that morning of almost Arctic weather.

The old walls and chimney stood for several years, mute and grim as a silent evidence of that devastating element -- FIRE. Finally in the early forties they were torn down and the bricks removed. During these years the farm was thrown out to a common and remained in that condition until purchased by Col. H.B. Fiddeman, in the first of the fifties, who occupied it for two years, when he sold out and went away. Who was the bonifide owner from 1860 to 1865, the writer is not prepared to say; but in the latter years it was bought by John W. Kirby, as his first venture in the purchase of real estate. In about two years Mr. Kirby sold it in two parcels, one to Albert Smith, the other to a Mr. Banks, both northern men. Smith worried along for awhile and failing to grow suddenly rich, sold out and departed; "a wiser and sadder man." He sold to William Saunders, a typical Englishman and a veritable "Johnnie Bull," who failed to get along peaceably with his neighbors; he likewise sold out and departed. It was next bought by John D. Bickel, since which time it has remained unsold. The larger portion of the tract, or the part bought by Mr. Banks, is still in the Banks family. It is the property of his daughter, Mrs. John D. Bickel, a surviving heir of Mr. Banks. This farm is in tenure of Mr. Nehemiah Kimmey, a veteran of the Civil War, and an honorable and upright citizen.

During the Centennial of the American Independence, a young man, George Ihrie by name, came to Delaware from Pennsylvania. He was a German by descent and a wagon builder by profession, and in the company with William Reynolds, a young blacksmith of Milton, built shops and began the business of wheelwrighting and blacksmithing. Ihrie married a young lady of Milton, a Miss Betts, and her brothers built a house for them near the shops. The business of the firm seemed to prosper for a while, but they soon dissolved partnership by selling out to Edward Atkins. Reynolds went to New York City and Ihrie moved to Milton. Mr. Atkins was a young man of sober and industrious habits, and soon won for himself, a reputation not only as a mechanic but as a citizen also. He also took a partner not in the shops, however, but in the housekeeping department. Mr. Atkins successfully conducted the business for a dozen years or more, and sold out to his brother-in-law, George W. Bennett, the present proprietor. Mr. Bennett is a thorough going man of middle age, sober, honest, and industrious, and is worth more to his country as an American citizen, than a score of the worthless sons of millionaires.

August 28, 1908

Next to the farm of Mrs. Samuel W. Kinder, situated on the Mispillion River, is the farm belonging to the heirs of the late George E. Davis-James P.L. Davis, Sallie M., Henry and Mark G.L. Davis, the three boys industrious, energetic and enterprising young men of Milford. They inherited it from their maternal grandfather, Dr. James P. Lofland, a well-known practicing physician of this vicinity more than half a century ago, who died in 1859 about sixty years of age. He was a cousin of Dr. John Lofland, the Milford Bard. His children were Hon. James R. Lofland, a member of Congress. and a prominent lawyer and politician; Dr. Mark Lofland, who adopted his father's profession and became prominent as a physician; Mary G., who became the wife of George E. Davis, and Peter L. Lofland, a retired merchant, the youngest one of the four children and the only one now living.

This is a fine farm possessing many possibilities, but unfortunately, like many other farms, it fell under the ban of that antiquated system -- life tenure -- a system which has too often proven the curse and bane of improvement and progress. The present owners however, being public spirited young men and having lately come into possession of it, will no doubt soon make it as desirable a farm in appearance and utility as any in this section. The soil is very susceptible, easily improved and well adapted to diversified farming. Fruit, vegetables and the cereals grow luxuriantly when plant-foods are properly applied. It is nicely located along the river and has a good landing from which produce may be shipped. To any young man with a liking for agricultural pursuits, it would be a fortune. The adjoining property, known as the Dr. Owens farm, is also a valuable piece of real estate. Many years ago it was owned by Dr. John P. Owens, who practiced medicine in Milford in the first half of the nineteenth century. After the death of Dr. Owens in 1844, the care of the farm devolved upon Frederick J. Owens, the oldest surviving one of his children, who took the farm in charge for a few years. Subsequently his brother Isaiah, who had now reached his majority, assumed control thereby releasing his brother Frederick, and affording him an opportunity to pursue his medical studies and attend lectures at the University of Pennsylvania. After graduating Dr. Frederick J. Owens located in Milford for a while, then went to Wilmington, and next located in Harrington, finally moving to Denton, Md., where he died in 1906 in the eighty-third year of his age. Isaiah Owens remained on the farm until the death of his mother, after which he left it and went to Illinois, for a period of several years. Returning he again resided on the farm but being of a roving disposition again became dissatisfied and took his departure. He was a very industrious hard working man but seemed to be unsuccessful in his undertakings. Whether living or dead the writer is not aware; if living he is now about eighty years of age.

Nehemiah Cole succeeded Mr. Owens as a tenant, and lived there many years. During the later years of Mr. Cole's occupancy, Dr. Owens erected new buildings and rendered his tenant and family more comfortable. On this farm Mr. Cole spent the greater portion of his married life, and reared a large family of children -- nine in number -- now all grown up and at work for themselves. Although he has seemed to miss that "tide in the affairs of men, which taken at its flood flows on to prosperity," he has won a reputation for honesty and uprightness that might well be envied by many men of less conscientious scruples.

Since the death of Dr. Owens, the farm which was almost a plantation, has been sold. It was bought by Short and Hall, hustling real estate dealers of Milford, who have divided it into three parcels and sold to other individuals. One part is now owned by Benjamin F. Davis, who will soon make it, if we are to judge by his former record, a profitable investment. Another portion is owned by Luther F. Cubbage who contemplates building upon it and clearing the land, which has never been broken. Before he accomplishes this task it is very probable that Mr. Cubbage will put many more ascriptions, on the stumps and roots in the land, than his illustrious namesake, Martin Luther, who nailed these on the church door of Wittenburg during the Reformation. Of the other parcel, the name of the purchaser has not yet been learned. Messrs. Short and Hall, properly considered, are public benefactors, by their system of buying large tracts of land and dividing it into smaller parcels, they make it possible for more men to become land owners and build homes for themselves and others that will not only make them independent and contented , but will add very greatly to the general prosperity of the country.

ISSAC R. JESTER
1909
COURTESY OF MILFORD CHRONICLE

January 22, 1909

The history of Milford Neck, if written by a abler pen than mine, would read like a romance. A complete story of its early traditions would seem very much like a fairy tail. Although there have been many accidents and episodes of which no definite description can be given and there are many others that ought to be preserved and handed down to prosperity, in a readable form. An intense desire to preserve and perpetuate the traditions is the apology the writer has to offer for this intrusion on the time and patience of the reader.

The territory on Milford Neck consists of a peninsula lying between Mispillon and Murderkill Rivers and extending from the headwaters of each river until the eastern boundary kisses the briny waters of the Delaware Bay. It has a coast line of more than ten miles in extent from the Mispillon to the Murderkill, fringed with a marshy skirting of about one mile in width, dotted with a number of small islands, which were formerly covered with a growth of large forest trees, magnificent and luxurient. Viewed from the Bay with the dense forest of timber on the main land for a background, it presents a picturesque and enchanting appearance to the beholder. It is little wonder that the early explorers bestowed on it the name of Paradise Point.

The early settlers of Milford Neck were mostly of English origin, with just enough Scotch and Irish blood in their veins to make them cheerful and contented and supply a wholesome amount of wit and humor for which their decedents have always been proverbial. They were in a large measure from the eastern shore of Maryland and Virginia and brought with them their manners and custom as well as their slaves. Their settlement in this section antedated the arrival of William Penn about two years. The grants of land which they patented from James the Duke of York dating back to 1680 about five years before he succeeded to the throne as James the second.

Among the early settlers are found such names as Bowman, Clark, Davis, Emerson, Hall, Fisher, Minors, Molleston, Manlove, Smith and Young whose decedents can be traced. The Harringtons of Milford and Mispillion Hundred very probable descended from James Harrington, the English Barrister and Patriot, who figured conspicuously in the reign of Cromwell and was compelled to flee from his country at the restoration of Charles II. Among the early settlers of this section was Henry Molleston. His real estate consisted of what is now known as the creamery farm owned by Dr. L.L. Carlisle, the farm of James A. Martin, a part of the farm of Thomas Kirby, 43 acres belonging to the heirs of Thomas Mason, the farm of the late John W. Hall Jr., and probably the two farms of Dr. William F. Goodwin, on the two last however I am not certain. Mr. Molleston was a man of much prominence, he was a member of the Assembly from 1698 to 1700, president of the Council from 1700 probably until his death which occurred about the time the three counties drew off from Pennsylvania and set up for themselves a separate organization. His large plantation passed to his son, Henry Molleston, who was also a very prominent man. After the death of Henry Mollestem (2nd) the estate passed to his son and daughter, Henry and Mary Molleston. The son, Henry Mollesten (3rd), receiving for his share all that part of the land on the north side of the road and extending to the Murderkill River and is still known as the Molleston farm. His sister Mary inherited that which lay on the south side of the road, each parcel containing more than six hundred acres. This Henry Molleston was a very prominent man in social and political circles, he owned slaves and was considered very wealthy. To most of his slaves he gave their freedom at his death. One of his slaves, Judith Molleston, the writer remembers distinctly; she could relate stories of the Revolution with a zest that made them interesting in the extreme; they so nearly corresponded with the stirring events of that period that their accuracy could not well be disputed. She died January, 1847, at the extreme age of ninety-one, out living her master nearly thirty years.

Henry Molleston was elected to many offices of trust and honor and faithfully discharged the duties of those offices. In 1799 he was elected as a member of the Legislature and held the office six years. He was County Treasurer 1805, State Treasurer in 1808, Member of the House of Representatives, 1813, State Senator, 1815 to 1817 and served as a speaker during the session of 1817. He was elected Governor in October 1819 and died in December of that year before his inauguration which would have taken place in January, 1820. For some years previous to his being elected Governor, he had been a resident of Murderkill Hundred instead of Mispillion as this Hundred was then called.

Sometime in the beginning of the eighteenth century the County of Kent was divided into Districts called Hundreds instead of Townships, and to that portion which we are describing was given the name Mispillion Hundred until 1823, when it was divided into two election districts; the western portion retaining the original name and the Eastern portion taking the name Milford Hundred. So powerful was the force of habit that many of the older citizens call it Mispillion Neck. It has also been dubbed Turkey Neck. Whether this title has been bestowed on account of the many luscious turkeys that are annually raised in this section or because of some fancied resemblance of the people to the inhabitants of the "sick man's dominion," has never yet been definitely settled; if the latter title is not very flattering.

January 29, 1909

Another large plantation in Milford Neck, which deserves special mention on account of its historical significance, is that tract of land known for nearly a hundred years as the "Polk Farm." It is supposed to have been patented by Mark Manlove about 1863, who came from England, first to Virginia, then to Delaware. It passed from him to his son, Matthew Manlove, by inheritance, and from him to Matthew Manlove (2nd) his son, who was a captain in Col. Samuel Petterson's Regiment Continental Army 1778. Captain Manlove's men saw hard service in the battles of Cowpens, Camden, Guilford's Court House and Hobkirks Hill, and was nearly annihilated in this Southern campaign, that the the shattered remanent was incorporated with Captain Robert Kirkwood's company.

This plantation of Captain Manlove, situated on the bay shore and open to the sea, was exposed to the insults, indignities and atrocities of a brutal British soldiery - always capable of any enormity. The very fact that being a patriot rendered his property and family less secure from British incursions. It was a common occurrence for them to forage his plantation, shoot down his cattle on the marshes and carry them away in their barges to their shipping that lay in the offing. Tradition informs us of an event that took place near this plantation, which is worthy of mention. During the war a Spanish Galleon was entering the bay freighted with specie for Philadelphis, consigned to Robert Morris, the financier of the Revolution. This money consisted of Spanish Milled Dollars and was securely fastened in iron-bound kegs and was being conveyed to the city for the benefit of the ragged, shoeless poorly fed by a British man-of-war ship, that was hovering around the capes of Delaware and was chased into the bay. To avoid being captured by their perusers, the captain and crew ran the Galleon aground, inshore from what is now known to sailors as Blade's Channel, and abreast of the farm of Matthew Manlove. In order to deprive the British from getting possession of this treasure, they threw the kegs overboard into the bay. Much of it was afterwards recovered and carried to a place of safety on the farm of Mr. Manlove. Some of it, however, was never recovered and it is said that many years afterwards a keg of this money was found by Lunn Manlove, an old slave, and taken by him to his home on Cabin Ridge. For the truthfulness of this story the writer can not vouch, but it is certain that several stray coins of this denomination have been found along the beach of this vicinity, in more recent times.

In early times the Manlove's in Mispillion Neck were numerous and influential. From 1700 to 1800, there were but few tracts of land lying along the Mispillion River, from its mouth to the New Wharf, that was not at sometime owned by some member of the Manlove family. This can be shown by the records in the offices of Register of Wills and Recorder of Deeds at Dover.

Several members of this family were prominent as holders of Public Offices. In 1734 George Manlove of Revolutionary fame, was collector of taxes for Mispillion Hundred, and it is a curious fact the real estate of all this vast territory is valued at less than $12,000 ($11,334.34) the amount of taxes being $193.15. It is wonderful to contemplate the great changes that have been wrought in this cycle of time. The increase in the value of real estate, including the towns that have grown up since that day, is simply enormous, probably aggregating at the present time more than one hundred million dollars. With now towns, few if any mills and no manufacturing establishments beyond the home circle, they style of living must have been very primitive indeed. And yet many of the citizens were wealthy-large land holders and the owners of many slaves which was, as we of the present generation see it, less a blessing than a curse.

February 5, 1909

Matthew Manlove (2nd) was the last of the Manlove family in Mispillion Neck. Jonathan Manlove, brother to Matthew, was sheriff of Kent County in 1804. Shortly after the income of the nineteenth century the name died out in this section, although the blood was transmitted and still exists in other names. Matthew Manlove was the maternal grandfather of the Hon. Charles Polk, twice Governor of Delaware, five times a member of the Legislature, president of the convention that formed the Constitution of 1832, of which John M. Clayton was a member and the leading spirit, Register of Wills from 1850 to 1853. He inherited the Homestead of his grandfather Matthew Manlove in the early part of the nineteenth century, and moved from Bridgeville to it in 1816, in the 28th year of his age.

The Manlove family was clearly connected with the Mollestons, the Brinckies, The Curtises, the Halls and the Purnelis of Mispillion Hundred, all of whom were very prominent in the political, financial and social circles.

The "Polk Farm" for the last hundred years has fared to be a paying investment. During the period it has been the theatre for the most lavish expenditure of money, of any farm in this section. When it came into the possession of Mr. Polk (1816) he straightaway began the erection of an elegant and costly mansion, which, when completed about 1820, was one of the most handsome and best equipped residences of its time in this part of Kent County. His next venture at improvement was the drainage of his low land and marshes. For this purpose he had erected a sluice or flume-way, through the beach into the bay. This consisted of a framework, planked with his heavy similar to the race way of a mill. It was about eight feet wide, the side walls averaging about five feet in depth to the bottom, with an automatic gate to repel the incoming tide. This contrivance worked well for a short time only. The excursions of the sea and the shifting of the sand soon filled it up bodily, and the experiment was a failure. In ten years hardly a vestige of this structure remained to be seen. In 1851 he made another attempt at drainage; this time by means of a culvert of trunk through the beach. It was a substantial frame work planed in on all sides, but its usefulness lasted but one winter, when it too was filled with sand from end to end by the action of the waves. This was the last experiment of the kind made by Mr. Polk.

In the early fifties, after a lapse of one hundred and fifty years, Governor Polk had this tract of more than eleven hundred acres re-surveyed, and it was found that by the encroachment of the sea it had lost one hundred and forty acres on the shore line; the length of this line being 320 perches, or just one mile, the average yearly wearing away was equal to 7 7/10 feet. This beach formerly known as "Sandy Inlet," as far back as the forties had the reputation of being the greatest "Front Fishery" along the shore. About 1843 the catching of these fish began to develop into a general business and men went into it as an occupation. Until well along in the fifties it was not a rare occurrence for one to land as many as one thousand bushels at a haul, but the climax has been reached, and of late years the quality has so decreased that the scarcity has made them almost a luxury.

This farm after remaining in the Polk family until nearly the close of the last century, was bought by William I. Simpson, who designed making it a stock and dairy farm of the first magnitude. If Mr. Simpson had requested us to paint a picture as an appropriate emblem of his success in the stock and dairy business, we should have painted a large horn with a man coming out of the little end. But after making a considerable outlay in building and other preparations for that purpose, Mr. Simpson, like the wise man in the Scripture, "foresaw the evil and hid himself," by selling out to Frank Greco, an Italian by birth and a Pennsylvanian by adoption who will most likely represent the other fellow who "passed on and was punished." Mr. Greco has started out with a lavish expenditure of money hitherto unknown in this section. His enterprise is certainly commendable especially so if it proves a success, but we are inclined to the opinion that he will never be able to render his lands of the Adriatic Peninsula - his native Italy. But he is a man of wonderful pluck and energy, financially about to carry out his designs. These characteristics are generally winning cards in the game of success. If he succeeds in establishing a system of drainage so as to render his land productive, and can repel the overflows so common to that section adjacent to the bay, he is alright; otherwise it is a doubtful experiment.

April 2, 1909

COL. JOHN WOOD

Few men in Milford Neck have figured more conspicuously in their day and generation than Col. John Wood. During the latter part of his life time he was the largest land owner in this vicinity, having in his possession more than two thousand acres of land. Among the dozen or more farms which he owned, were included some of the largest and best. Nor did his wealth consist in real estate alone; he owned much vessel property which he employed between here and Philadelphia. He also owned many slaves, which were used in the cultivation of his land. In addition to this he was a speculator in such produce as the country afforded, grain, wood, bark, and slaves.

Of the early history of Col. Wood but little is known. Whence he came or what time is uncertain. It is known however that he was located in this vicinity as early as the close of the Revolutionary War, and must have been a young man at the time. He married Mary Molleston, sister of Henry Molleston, Esq., who brought of him a dower more than a thousand acres of land, several slaves and some ready money. Whether he brought such wealth with him is not known, but the presumption is that he did not; that he possessed the rare faculty of winning the confidence of his fellow man, and appropriating the confidence to his own advantage was manifest.

He was a man of medium height, moderately well proportioned form, sharp angular features, with deep penetrating eyes. His business life began with the founding of the nation. The young Republic had just emerged from a long and desperate struggle which had paralyzed nearly all business and destroyed a great deal of property. Active energetic men like Col. Wood were a necessity for the development of the country. Enervated and discouraged by the war, with the finances at a low ebb and with his heavy debts hanging over them, many men were ready to despair, at the gloomy prospect. Not so with Col. Wood, seeing his opportunity, he embraced it with a fervor peculiar to his nature and made use of it to such an extent that he soon became the leading man in the section, in a business point of view. His astute business qualifications, coupled with his already growing wealth placed him in the forefront of citizenship, in this community. As his wealth increased he invested the surplus in land, which owing to the depressed condition of the times, he could buy for a song (figuratively speaking) and pay for by whistling half of the tune. In a few years Col. Wood became one of the largest land holders in Milford Neck, and was recognized as the wealthiest and most influential citizen. Such was his unbounded influence over the people, that virtually he held them in the palm of his hand and no enterprise could be undertaken without his approval. Although the people had but recently been relieved of the shackles that bound them, they were ready to submit to the overwhelming influence of this master mind.

In view of the fact of his great popularity it is a matter of surprise that he never once was sent to represent his people in the Halls of Legislature. Perhaps it was because he did not aspire to public office, his business being more remunerative.

The darkest shadow in the background of the picture of Col. Wood's life, was his unlimited avarice, but with all his craving for worldly store he was a philanthropist and a patriot. His patriotism was demonstrated by the mustering of a Battalion of men for the defense of the State in the War of 1812 and marching with them to the relief of Lewistown, when besieged by the British. The Battallion was recruited by his endeavor and equipped largely at his expense. On the farm now owned by Charles Kirby, then belonging to Col. Wood, was a large field, for many years out to a "common" which was used for drilling his men and was long afterwards known as "Muster field." It is probable that this is the period in which he won his military title.

His philanthropy is shown by his liberality to all benevolelent purposes. The first M.E. Church in Milford Neck was erected through his generosity. He donated the land which it was built and was the principal contributor to its erection. It was a wooden structure built in 1790 and stood for sixty years in honor of its founder. He was not only benevolent in the deeds of public character but also in the minor acts, where the "left hand knoweth not what the right hand doeth." A story is told of him that fully illustrates this principal. On one occasion, a colored man in his employ, as captain of one of his vessels, was stricken with smallpox. Leaving his vessel at one point in the Mispillion River, he went to the residence of Col. Wood, a mile or more away, in the still hours of the night and called for assistance, stating his condition at a proper distance from the house. Col. Wood answered his call from the window, directed him to a vacant house near by, and told him to make himself comfortable as possible until morning when his needs would be properly attended to. In the early morning Col. Wood summoned a physician, procured a nurse, and the man passed safely through that terrible disease, living many years afterward to tell the story.

The will of Col. Wood gives unmistakable evidence of his generous nature. A considerable portion of his estate was given to those who were in now wise connected with him by ties of consanguinity, but were worthy objects of his beneficence. One redeeming trait in his character was the manumission of all his slaves; those that were under twenty one he gave their freedom when they arrived of age. His solicitous care for his mother, who survived him, is another evidence of his character. He provided that she should be carefully and comfortably maintained during her life, and bound his entire estate, real and personal, for that purpose. He left no children, his only daughter, Catherine Wood, married Charles Stewart, a jeweler, of Philadelphia, and became the mother of two children, John and Aaron Stewart, who were small boys when their mother died and were taken care of by their grandfather. For their maintenance and education he provided amply and also left them considerable of his estate, they being his only lineal descendants. His first wife dying in the meridian of her life, he married Mary Hall, daughter of Winlock Hall, and aunt of the late ex-Governor John Wood Hall. Of this marriage there was no issue.

Col Wood died in September, 1818 about fifty seven years of age, and was buried in the shadow of the church which he had founded. His remains rested there in an unmarked grave for ninety years. Recently, however, Mrs. Sarah Hall Lister of Philadelphia, daughter of Governor Hall, and a benevolent lady, has had a very imposing monument with a suitable inscription to his memory placed upon his grave. This is a very praiseworthy deed in Mrs. Lister, and one for which the entire community owes her their gratitude.

INDIANS

The earliest known inhabitants of Delaware were the Indian tribe of the Lenni-Lanape, which means "Original People" or "Natives," and were one of the most advanced and civilized tribes in the Eastern United States. The other members of the Algonkian language family respectfully called them the "grandfathers." The men were tall in stature with broad shoulders, narrow waists, broad-high cheek bones, skin of rusty brown color, and straight black hair.

The Lenni-Lenape were an intelligent, proud and fair-minded people. They were considered to be skillful workers and good quick marksmen. William Penn noted "they tread softly - and mostly walk with a lofty chin - and whose wives were true servants of the husbands" (from Lindestrom's "Geographia America").

Their houses were an oval frame work of poles bent in a dome shape and covered with slab of elm bark or similar material. Although we might not think of them as gourmets, it seems they were very good cooks having many and varied recipes plus skillfully regulating their fires and selecting the proper kind of woods for the various dishes.

Pow-wow's were very important to their way of life. When the chief was confronted with a problem the men of the tribe gathered around a large fire for a Pow-wow. While the women prepared food, the elders deliberated and the calumet (lighted pipe) was passed around to help meditation.

Although they planted maize and some vegetables, they were mainly hunters. This area, being one huge primeval forest, was probably the southern most point of their hunting area.

The Lenni-Lenape peaked in their glory about 1700 when they were ruled by Chief Tamanend. After coming under the domination of the Iroquois in 1720 their spirit was broken. As time passed, they moved further west and by 1800 most of them had moved to Missouri, later to Kansas and finally they settled in Oklahoma in 1868.

Today we sometimes hear the Lenni-Lenape referred to as the "Delaware" Indians. It seems a shame that the heritage of these people could not have been locally preserved.

EARLY SETTLERS

Henry Hudson, English explorer, most likely was the first white man to visit the Delaware region. In his ship "Half Moon" he sailed into Delaware Bay in 1609 searching for a passage to the Far East. Seeing the bay led to a river he left the region and sailed northward.

Captain Samuel Argall of the colony of Virginia, seeking shelter from a storm, used the bay for refuge in the same year. He named it the De La Warr Bay in honor of the governor of Virginia, Lore de la Warr.

The first settlement was started when the Dutch landed at Swandendael (Zwaanendael), now Lewes, in the year 1631. For some reason an Indian tribe, still unknown, destroyed the fort and massacred the settlers. The area was resettled in 1659.

In 1638 a boatload of colonists, consisting of Swedes, Finns and Livonians, landed at Paradise Point (Clark's Point) in what is now Milford Neck. They did not make a permanent settlement but, after staying a short while, went up the Delaware to "The Rocks" (present site of Wilmington) and made the first permanent settlement in the State. The Swedish settlers introduced the first log cabins in America to Delaware.

A Royal Charter, by King Charles II of England, granted the Delaware Counties to his brother James, the Duke of York, in 1664. This was the start of the English rule.

William Penn, famous English Quaker, set up a colony in America which eventually became the State of Pennsylvania. It seems Penn's father, at this point deceased, was owed an unpaid debt, with interest, of $80,000 by Charles II. Penn asked the king to repay the debt with wilderness land in America. So on March 4, 1681 the king issued a charter granting the territory west of the Delaware River between New York and Maryland.

Penn was a man of vision, spirituality and idealism and possessed a love for his fellow man. His early dealings with the Indians reflected his love of equality and fair play. He said "Whatever sober and free men can reasonable desire for the security and improvement of their own happiness, I shall heartily comply with."

In March, 1681 William Penn began prolonged negotiations with the Duke of York to turn over the Lower Counties (Delaware) to him thereby insuring Pennsylvania access to the ocean. After much procrastination, the Duke finally granted the area to Penn in August, 1682.

Penn granted a character of liberties to the "Three Lower Counties" permitting them to elect their own legislative assembly, enjoying similar privileges and rights which were established for the parent colony.

Penn visited his colony only twice. In October, 1682, he saw his colony for the first time. While here he made a treaty with the Indians and got the colony well started before his return to England in August, 1684. His only other visit was in December, 1699 to settle some problems that had arose in the colony and rewrite the constitution to meet the new needs of the people. He returned to London in February, 1701 where he lived until his death in 1718.

After a series of quarrels, Delaware assemblymen, in 1704, asked permission to hold separate assembly which was granted. This gradually widened the legislative separation although Pennsylvania governors continued to govern these counties until the Revolutionary War.

The counties we now know as Kent and Sussex were not always called this. In 1860 the Whorekill court divided Kent County into the southern half of Deale County, now called Sussex, and St. Jones County. On 17 December 1682 an Act of Union annexed the three Lower Counties to Pennsylvania and St. Jones was changed back to Kent County.

Delaware even today is the only state which divides its counties into "hundreds." Hundreds have no government of their own but serve as a basis for taxation and representation. Mispillion Hundred, which was a vast forest of oak and pine, was where the early grants designated the property lay. An Act of Assembly on the 28 January 1830 divided Mispillion Hundred using a road formerly used by the "Philadelphia, Dover and Norfolk Steamboat and Transportation Company" as a dividing line. West of the road would be Mispillion Hundred and east of the road would be Milford Hundred. This made the boundaries for Milford hundred as below:

Eastern .... Delaware Bay
Southern .... Mispillion Creek
Western .... Mispillion Hundred
Northern .... Murderkill Creek

LAND GRANTS

The early grants were issued by the Whorekill Court which was appointed by William Penn. This area was a very popular area and many grants were issued for land here in 1680. A number of those are listed below:

Peter Baucom	600	acres
William Troth	200	acres
Thomas Williams	200	acres
John Briggs	400	acres
Richard Williams	600	acres

The name of Baucombrig Creek probably came about because the properties of Peter Baucom and John Briggs bordered on both sides of the creek.

In tracing back my own property I have found that it was part of Richard Williams 600 acres which he called "Williams Choice." Richard Williams also owned another 544 acres which was called "Anglefield,"

There was another grant in 1680 to John Betts. This grant was for a tract which began at the bay north of Baucombrig Creek and ran all the way to what is now the Thompsonville Church. It paralleled the creek being better than 1/2 mile wide and 3 3/10 miles long and amounted to 1000 acres.

John Briggs, although owning land in Milford Hundred probably never lived here. The census records indicate he lived near St. James Creek, was a planter and had four children.

Peter Baucom was appointed and served for many years as sheriff of Kent County.

At this point I have included another article by Isaac R. Jester which explains some landmarks names and how some last for many years even though surroundings change.

April 16, 1909

OLD LANDMARKS

It is a strange fact, though a matter of much surprise, how long names will stick to certain places. On one of the farms of Col. Robert H. Williams, in Milford Neck, there is a small branch or brooklet that rises and flows in a southeasterly direction until it falls into Crooked Gut, a small tributary of Mispillion River. This miniature stream still bears the patronymic of "Perry's Branch." The land was patented and held by William Perry, previous to 1865. For more than a hundred years the name of the Perrys have not existed in this locality, and yet that small stream has borne the name for more than two centuries and will perhaps continue for centuries to come.

Another stream, flowing into the Mispillion River, known as "Beaver Dam Branch," has held that title ever since the land was patented in 1861. This stream furnishes a theme for thought and reflection. At a point where the public road crosses the stream may yet be seen a part of the dam; the work of that industrious and intelligent little animal - the beaver. On the north side of the road, above the dam, is a pond two to three feet deep and extending over an area of about a half acre unquestionably, the work of that sagacious animal. The pond, formerly abounding with fishes, is slowly filling in with silt and rubbish forming the upper stream and has to some extent become a stagnant pool; but Nature, which makes but few mistakes, in order to abate the nuisance, has planted it in flowers - the beautiful and highly-prized water lily. Many persons traveling along the highway pass this relic of antiquity unheeded, never realizing that it was once the home of the fur bearing animal, which has long ago been driven away by the incoming tide of civilization. Many generations have passed away, and have been forgotten, but evidence of those skillful little creatures still remain. And now comes the question: "How long will earths works endure?"

Seventy years ago, when every farmer's home was a factory for the manufacture of clothing for the family, this pond was utilized by them for the rotting of flax. It was subjected to this treatment until the woody portion became soft, and by means of the flaxbrake could be separated from the fiber, which was spun into thread. To most of the present generation this procedure is a lost art and a flaxbrake an instrument unknown.

Just how long the public road leading through this section has been in use is uncertain. It may have been open when the Steward kings ruled England. Certain it is, that it was in use when the Colonies were governed by a king. A certain part of the road, where it crosses "Love Long Branch," is known as "Kings Causeway," perhaps being named in honor of the king - not much of a compliment either.

The stream known as Molleston's Branch has borne this name for many years - perhaps as far back as the early settlement. The land on the eastern side having been patented by a man of that name it was held by his descendents until 1820 when it passed out of the family and the name in this section became nearly extinct, but the stream of water still retains its original name.

On the farm once owned by the Molleston's, but now the property of Dr. Lester L. Carlisle, stands an old time building; one time this was the homestead of the Molleston's. How long it has stood there no one knows, but it has bravely defied the wastes of time and is today in a good state of preservation. It has several times been repaired but the design and general outline has been sacredly preserved. The architecture is of colonial style.

Still another point of interest on the Murderkill River is "Cole's Shoal," where the river touches the main land. It took its name from a former owner, Spencer Cole, who owned the land as long ago as the beginning of the eighteenth century and still bears his name. Nearly three fourths of a century ago it was a great business place; a store was kept by the owner, Aaron Bowman, that did a large volume of business. Grain, wood, bark, and staves were bought and shipped to Philadelphia in immense quantities. Later these activities ceased; the place has fallen into a state of "disrepair" and its former glory has departed, but the name still remains.

Next comes "Lowbar's Landing" which has borne the name for many generation. Improvements in navigation on the river has isolated these places from the main line of water travel and thrown them in the background.

Further down the river is "Barren Island" (corrupted into Barn Island). Surrounded by a large body of marsh, this island skirts the river-side and contains about three acres. The romance of this island almost equals Irving's "Legend of Sleepy Hollow." Apart from its weird and otherwise picturesque appearance its notoriety consists in the fabulous stories that were once told of its hidden treasures. According to the story Captain William Kidd, a freebooter, sailed into the river and buried his booty, consisting of specie, on the island. There is little evidence that Captain Kidd frequented the waters of the Delaware Bay, much less one of its small tributaries. But the fact remains that in previous years the "Divining Rod" and digging utensils have been used extensively on this island in quest of Kidd's gold. The advance of science and the uplift of intelligence have pretty well cured the present generation of such ridiculous delusions. It has been demonstrated with certainty, however, that there are hidden treasures within six inches of the surface in many places in Milford Neck, that may readily be obtained by persistent systematic cultivation of the soil.

Situated on the land of William G. Hering, Esq., in Milford Neck, there is another relic of the olden time, which may be interesting to the reader. It is known as the "Troy's Cave" and is located in a dense swamp, and even at this day it is almost unapproachable. Its dimensions are about eight feet in width and about twelve feet long, with an arched roof sufficiently high for a man six feet in stature to stand erect. Both ends are open, whether by design or otherwise, cannot be determined, as many years have passed since its construction. Evidently it must have been erected for the purpose tradition ascribes to it - a place for a concealment for the Tories, to escape the wrath of the patriots. Few men now living know of this cave, but it still exists, a mute monument - somber and grim - to the times that tried men's souls - the American Revolution. Such is the story, briefly told, of the Tory's Cave," nor is it an idle vaporing of an imaginative brain.

BIOGRAPHICAL SKETCHES FROM EARLY YEARS

This information for this section was obtained primarily from Volumes I & II of Biographical and Genealogical History of the State of Delaware, 1899, Published by J.M. Runk & Co.

I also looked up records in the Recorder of Wills and the birth and death records at the Hall of Records to update this portion of my sketches. Most of the people in these sketches are mentioned through out this book either in the writings of Isaac R. Jester or in my accounts of early life in Milford Neck.

It is my hope that this section will bring some of the people of this area a little more to life for you as you read through the other chapters.

JOSHUA BENNETT

BORN: 08/25/1822   DIED: 04/10/1912

Parents: Joshua II and Mary (Malloy) Bennett
Married: 06/29/1947 to Ruth Jane (daughter of Clement & Mary [Shockley] Houston)

Joshua & Ruth Jane's children: Mary A. born 07/05/1848 (died in infancy), Eliza Jane born 1850 (first married John M. Webb & second John Andrew), John H. born 05/22/1852 (married Elizabeth Mills), Joseph C. born 04/1854 (married Emeline Macklin), Joshua IV born 01/24/1856 (married Anna Parsons), Anna M. born 07/20/1858 (married Edward Atkins), Mary L. born 05/09/1860 (married Albert Webb), George H. born 06/24/1866 (married Harriet A. Short)

Joshua owned the National P. Luff farm which contained 200 acres. He lived on this farm until 1886 when he purchased a dwelling and moved into Milford. He still continued to manage all his farms and also found the time to serve an uncompleted term in the Delaware Legislature when Governor Watson retired from that office. Joshua's wife, Ruth Jane, was born 02/01/1827 and lived till 07/16/1893.

ROBERT JOHN BESWICK

BORN: 07/07/1834   DIED: 04/19/1907

Great-grandparents: John and Phoebe (daughter of Matthew and Mary Manlove) Brinckloe

Grandparents: Curtis Brinckloe and Sarah S. (Purnell) Beswick

Curtis & Sarah's children: John Edward born 08/06/1826 died 08/10/1827, William Purnell born 01/07/1830 (married William G. Hemming of Milford), Robert John, Sarah Ann born 02/14/1838 (married Hezekiah Mustin), George Washington Purnell born 03/22/1841 died 10/20/1854 and Mary Elizabeth born 03/04/1845 died 10/04/1845.

Robert attended school and worked on the family farm until 1874. At this time he left the homestead and became a justice of the peace and notary public in Milford, DE. A venture where he invested in the schooner "Allie B. Cathrall" did so well he built or bought an interest in six other vessels. When the home farm was divided his share was 185 acres to which he later added 150 adjoining acres. The management of his vessels and real estate kept his time fully occupied. He also served many offices is Milford government, was a stockholder in the First National Bank of Milford, a Levy Court commissioner from 1891 - 1985 and was President of the Milford Ice-house Company.

WILLIAM PURNELL BESWICK

BORN: 01/07/1828   DIED: 06/12/1892

Father: Curtis Brinkley (Brinklue) Beswick

Mother: Sallie Purnell

Married 12/20/1860   Susan Elizabeth (born to William Slaughter in Queen Annes Cty, MD and reared in West Dover Hrd., Kent Cty, DE)

William & Susan's children: Sallie May born on 01/06/1862 (Mrs. John F. Hammond), Anna Purnell born 06/16/1863, William George born 05/08/1865 (died young), John Brinkley born 06/11/1867, William Purnell & Edward Slaughter twins born 11/26/1868 (William died at age nine and Edward married Harriet Emma Jackson, daughter of Rev. Louis H. Jackson) and Thomas Clausen born 10/14/1876 (moved to Philadelphia and opened a dental office).

William was born in Milford Neck, Kent Cty, DE. He began a teaching career at an early age and taught in Milford and elsewhere for twenty-five years. He resided with his father assisting in the management of the farm. After the death of his father he continued dividing his time between teaching and running the farm. Ten years after his marriage he relinquished his profession and gave full attention to the farming operation. William's wife, Susan E., was born 05/28/1837 and out lived him by twenty-eight years. She passed on 08/06/1920.

JOHN CLEMENT CLIFTON

BORN 04/21/1851   DIED: 00/00/1926

Grandfather: Clement Clifton

Father: Daniel born 10/22/1811 in the "Forest" (Milford Neck)

Mother: Mary Anne born 1809 (daughter of John and Prisailla [Ward] Cathel)

Daniel & Mary's children: Sarah (married Nathaniel Cole), Angeline (married James H. Kirby) & John Clement

Married on 5/31/8176 Eliza Jane born 09/22/1854 to William Henry and Sarah Ann (Downs) Richards

John & Eliza Jane's children: H.D., William Howard, Elizabeth, John W., James ira, Josephine and Kenneth Richards

John grew up in Milford Neck and until age nineteen attended the Pine Grove school. After a term in a private school in Milford, DE he returned to Pine Grove school to launch a teaching career. He taught there for eight years and then moved on to Oak Grove for several years, Milwood school, Bennett's Gate school and a school in the Cedarfield district. After his father died he became a successful farmer by taking over and eventually purchasing the homestead. Eliza Jane died in 1938, out living her husband by thirteen years.

WILLIAM PRIMROSE CULLEN

BORN: 03/24/1834   DIED: 00/00/0000

Grandparents: Hesekiah and Elizabeth Cullen

Father: James P. born 01/12/1801

Mother: Sarah Primrose (parents: Elias and Amelia)

Married on 10/04/1870 in Frederica to Caroline (daughter of Hesekiah & Harriet Rogers)

William and Caroline's children: Arthur B. born 02/28/1871 (married Susan Wilkinson in Wilmington), Edith Clark born 07/20/1873, Clara Mabel born 03/06/1876, Lydia D. born 03/21/1878 & Harriet born 02/14/1880

William remained on the farm during his youth and attended the neighborhood public schools. After that he engaged in the stove and tinware business in Frederica for three years. He then went to Snow Hill, Md and opened a similar mercantile business for eleven years. He then returned to Milford in October 1883 and continued in business for ten years until his health compelled him to give up his trade. He was appointed Justice of the Peace and Notary Public in 1886 and reappointed in 1893.

CHARLES H. FITZGERALD

BORN: 05/15/1853   DIED: 00/00/0000

Grandparents: George and Elizabeth Fitzgerald

Father: Ezekiel born: 03/29/1819 died: 03/17/1878

Mother: Elizabeth Mills

Married on 11/12/1888 in Camden, NJ to Anna L. (daughter of James and Ann [Taylor] Anderson)

Charles and Anna's child: Mary Paine born 07/09/1897

Charles was born and spent his first fifteen years in Milford Hrd. He attended school and worked on the home farm. His schooling was completed in Cedar Creek Hrd. in Sussex County where he farmed until 1883. He then moved to Wilmington and was employed by Jackson & Sharp Company for eleven years. It was at this time that he established the Ideal Art School.

JOHN S. HERRINGTON

BORN: 02/04/1825   DIED: 00/00/1888

Grandfather: Abner - native of Mispillion Hrd.

Abner's children: Benjamin, William, Abner II, Moses, Harriet, Ruth, Nimrod, David & Sarah

Father: Abner II - born: Mispillion Hrd. died 1845

Mother: Elizabeth Sattersfield (father: William Sattersfield)

Abner II's children: Ann, Sarah (Mrs. Peter Harrington), Levi (moved to Kansas), William, Martin, Charles, David (moved to Pennsylvania), Elias (moved to Minnesota), John S. & Elizabeth
Married in 1855 to Caroline (daughter of Carry & Lydia Frazier)

John S. & Caroline's children: Edward F., Hugh Miller (became postal worker in Jersey City, IL), Annie L., Carrie (Mrs. John Collier), John S. Jr (moved to Princeton, NJ) & Fannie S.

John S. Herrington attended the old country school and had as one of his teachers William Sharp. After his father's death he managed the Mispillion farm until his mother's death in 1845. He then turned the operation of the farm over to Elias and started clerking at John William's store in Milford.   In 1846 he moved to Odessa where he stayed for four years.   At that time he started his frontier journey to New York, Ohio, Michigan, Illinois, Iowa and Missouri. In November of 1851 he returned to Delaware and started a mercantile business at Fork Landing. The purchase of a 183 acre farm took place at this same time but he did not build his home on it till 1853. He was elected county commissioner in 1866 and served two four year terms.   John moved to Dover, after turning over the farm to his son, in 1882. He was later elected Sheriff of Kent County and served his full term before dying in 1888.

BENJAMIN F. HUDSON

BORN: 1858   DIED: 1929

Father: Jonas S. born near Williams, Sussex Cty, DE

Mother: Rachel Davis

Married on 02/06/1882 to Mary E. (daughter of John R. & Naomi [Dickerson] Maloney) by Rev. J.B. Quigg

Benjamin & Mary had a daughter T., in 1885 who died in infancy

Benjamin went to school and farmed in his early years, taking over a full share of the farm work at age twenty-two. He later went to Philadelphia, PA and shipped out as a mate on the steamship "Pennsylvania" which was bound for Liverpool, England. After making one voyage he returned to Milford Neck where he remained until January 9, 1881. He rented Mrs. Talbot's farm for ten years and then purchased Mrs. Margaret Ackerman's farm which contained 147 acres.

Mary E. Benjamin's wife, was born in 1858 and died in 1943 at eighty five years of age.

MAJOR JESTER

BORN AND DIED IN CEDAR NECK HUNDRED, SUSSEX CTY, DE

Married: Mary Deputy

Their children: All but two died while very young, Benjamin E. born 07/01/1827 (married Rachel D. Webb) & Rachel (married Absalom Hill)

Major, farmer and teacher, was a native of the Eastern Shore of Maryland. His daughter, Rachel and her new husband moved to Milford Neck where they eventually built and ran what is now called the "Thompson Store." His son Benjamin was a very successful farmer and at one point owned a 100 acre farm in Ellendale, a 44 acre farm in Nanticoke Hundred and a small farm at New Market. Benjamin also owned several lots and two valuable houses in Ellendale.

ANDREW J. MALONEY

BORN: 02/18/1830   DIED: 04/24/1912

Grandfather: William Maloney (resided in Sussex Cty, DE)

Father: John Maloney born 1803

Mother: Mary Thompson of Kent County, DE

John & Mary's children: Sarah E. (married Thursten Mason of Chester, PA), William T. (married Sarah A. Dyer of Lebanon, DE), Andrew J., Susan (married J. Wesley Kirby), John Robert (married Naomi Dickerson) & Caroline (married Joseph A. Clendaniel of Wisconsin).

John's second marriage after Mary's death was to Ann Holland of Milford Neck.

Andrew married 07/08/1852 to Sarah E. Butler of Farmington by Rev. T.P. McColley in Sussex County

Andrew & Sarah's children: Robert (died early manhood), Eugenie (died early womanhood), Sarah, Alexander, Andrew Jackson, Cora & Carrie (all died in their youth), William E. (married Mary Matilda Smith), Angline (married George Davis), Willard S. (married Catherine Ingram) & John T. (married Sarah Evans).

Sarah E., Andrews wife was born 02/03/1833 and lived until 12/10/1913.

Andrew was born on the Beswick farm in Milford Hundred. As a boy he resided on different farms because his father would rent first one and then another. At age twenty-one he married and leased a farm for several years. He saved and purchased the Nathaniel Hickman farm and made many improvements.

JOHN ROBERT MAHONEY

BORN: 10/24/1834   DIED: 04/22/1908

Parents: John & Mary (Thompson) Maloney

Married: 02/18/1855 Naomi A. (daughter of Benjamin & Nancy L. (Webb) Dickerson

John and Naomi's children: I. Lorena (married Henry Hudson - died young), Josephine born 06/10/1857 (married Henry Hudson), Mary E. born 12/21/1858 (married B. Hudson), James Robert II born 08/11/1862 (married Mary Higman), Jenny Lind born 01/09/1865 (married James Sipple - had two children: Sarah E. & Naomi), Willam G. born 06/13/1866 (married Mary Ingraham), Robert H. born 04/08/1868 (died in infancy), TWINS born 05/31/1870 Thomas J. (married Bertha French) and Andrew J. (married Mary Scott) & Eliza R. born 02/18/1874.

John's wife, Naomi, who was born 12/09/1832 died on 10/11/1895. Both of their graves are in Odd Fellows cemetery in Milford, Delaware.

John was born on the Beswick farm but after one year they moved to Revel's Landing Farm. His education took place in the school house that originally was the first M.E. Church in Thompsonville. After his marriage he leased the Hickman farm for eighteen years. He then farmed on two separate farms belonging to Robert H. Williams. He was elected assessor of Milford Hundred for one term.

DICKERSON MORRIS MEREDITH

BORN: 04/11/1800

DIED: 06/15/1893

Father: William T. Meredith

Marriages: William's first wife was a Morris; children: Mary (Mrs. Davenport) & Dickerson Morris - William's second wife was a Stafford; children: Esther (Mrs. James Rawley) & Peter (married Amanda Temper) - William's third wife was a Young; children: Sarah (Mrs. George Fitzgerald), John (married Amelia Parsons), Daniel (married Elizabeth Haming), Henry (became an MD in Maryland), Lydia (Mrs. Edward Quillen) & Hugh (married Caroline Wilkinson).

Dickerson was born in Sassafras, New Castle County, DE and moved to Milford Hundred with his father while still a child. He was married April 22, 1852 to Sallie A., who was born 02/1/1816 and died 05/04/1897, by the Rev. W.L. Gray. Dickerson owned a large tract of land in Milford Neck and was a very efficient farmer. He was very interested in public affairs and did much in the community. He was an active member of the M.E. Church of Thompsonville.

BENJAMIN COVINGTON NEEDLES

BORN: 10/27/1849   DIED: 00/00/1929

Grandfather: John - blacksmith with shop in Milford Neck

Grandmother: Mary Poynter of Sussex County

Father: John P. born 1827 died 1877

Mother: Mary Covington died 1880

John P. and Mary were very active in the Sardis ME Church

Benjamin learned agricultural work early in life and then learned the masonry profession. He lived with his father until he reached majority, at which time he visited relatives out West where he worked as a mason for two and one half years in Milton Township, Cass County, Michigan. He spent another year in a brickyard in Indiana before returning home and, with his brother Theodore, purchased the 80 acre homestead and took up farming.

CHARLES CHRISTOPHER SHORT

BORN: 04/10/1844   DIED: 00/00/1929

Father: John Short born 1807 in Smyrna

Mother: Sarah Hendrickson

John and Sarah's children: Samuel (married Letitia Emory and moved to Bridgeton, NJ, (Mary Ellen (married Selby Thompson), James H. married Mary Smith and moved to Bowers), Elizabeth (married Abraham Bunn and moved to Lebanon, PA and Edward H. (married Mame Griffity)

John Short died in Milford Neck on the homestead in 1892

Married on 12/20/1868 Mary Frances (daughter of Samuel and Louise [Edgehill] Cubbage) who was born 1846 and died 1919

Charles and Mary Frances' children: Edward H. born 12/12/1872, Sarah L. born 02/01/1876 and Ira born 09/01/1882

Charles was in Company "C" of the 1st Delaware Cavalry form 1861 to 1865. Afterwards he spent three years on the homestead farming with his father. He then opened a store in Bowers Beach which he ran for three years. At this point he went back into farming by leasing the Potter farm in Milford Neck for nine years. He then went to Cedar Neck and farmed for eight years and in 1888 purchased a 64 acre farm in Lewes and Rehoboth Hundred.

DANIEL ALEXANDER THOMPSON

BORN: 01/09/1840   DIED: 09/24/1990

PARENTS: JAMES AND SARAH (POWELL) THOMPSON

MARRIAGE: 1st wife Mary E. M. Jester (daughter of Major Jester) married on 01/16/1869 by Rev. Jonathan Willis. Mary died 12/17/1869 after giving birth to one child, Mary E., who was born 12/01/1869 and died 07/17/1871

His second wife Lydia Annie was born 03/23/1844 to Thomas R. and Lydia (Houston) Wilson and she died on 11/28/1917. Her marriage to Daniel A. took place on 01/01/1873.

CHILDREN of Daniel and Lydia:

1) a son, Harvey Alexander born 03/19/1875 - married Eliza R. was born 02/14/1882 to David C. and Amanda J. (Minner) Stevenson and she died 03/19/1949; Harvey A. died 07/26/1868

2) a daughter, Sarah Virginia born 06/28/1877 - married on 12/25/1920 Wilbur Edward Mills (born 09/15/1864 - died 08/17/1937) married her second husband on 04/14/1946 Hamilton Lewis Patterson (born 03-18-1873 - died 07/21/1957) Sarah V. died 09/19/1969. Neither Harvey or Sarah had any children.

JAMES THOMPSON

BORN: 1804   DIED: 07/17/1869

Mother: Margaret Thompson

Married: 02/21/1833 to Sarah Powell (daughter of Zadoc and Caty Powell)

James and Sarah's children: Ann Eliza born 03/06.1864 died 03/11/1866; Andrew born 03/03/1836 died 10/26/1836; James Henry born 09/13/1837 (married 02/02/1866 to Georganna Morris of Chester, PA) died 12/30/1873; Daniel Alexander born 01/09/1842 (married Lydia Annie Wilson) died 09/13/1866; Joshua H. born 04/11-1845 died 04/03/1879; Mary E. born 12/15/1849 died 07/20/1851

ZADOK POWELL

Married: Caty

Children: Nancy born 01/02/1789 died 02/26/1873; Thomas born 09/28/1791; William born 03/02/1799; Robert born 03/16/1796; Rachel born 03/02/1799; Sarah born 06/25/1804 (married James Thompson) died 01/01/1866; Zadok born 04/16/1802 and Sally born 08/02/1910

Robert Powell and his wife, Alice, had as children Mary Ann born 03/05/1802 and Elizabeth born 09/18/1823

JOHN WESLEY COLLINS WEBB

BORN: 05/04/1810   DIED: 01/22/1902

Grandfather: Dorman Webb from Sussex County

Parents: Sylvester and Sarah (Argo) Webb

Married on 05/13/1834 to Sarah Ann (daughter of Henry and Nancy (Spence) Davis

John and Sarah's children: James Henry born 03/29/1835 (married Annie F. Thompson), Margaret Ann born 08/04/1837 (married Lyston Houston), Sarah Elizabeth born 06/18/1839 (married James Jester), John Mitchell born 10/18/1841 (married Jane Bennett), Rachel Caroling born 02/22/1845 (married Edward Sipple), Charles Alexander born 10/25/1848 (married Jennie Morris), Sylvester born 04/23/1850 (died at age three), May Marie born 11/18/1852, Amanda Ottilia Kelley born 02/19/1856 (married David Isaacs) and Francis Albert born 02/22/1883 (married Mary L. Bennett and had three children: Ethel, Arthur and Francis Albert II).

BAPTIST CHURCH

Although early records of the Baptist Church in this vicinity are lost and the church was never numerically strong, it is still a part of this sections history.

The first building devoted exclusively to Baptist worship undoubtedly was the "Old Baptist Meeting House" three miles North of Milford in Milford Neck. It was probably erected in the mid 1700's. Authentic information shows building repairs of the type usually needed in 30 to 40 years, such as a new roof, were performed in 1796. The building seemed to be devoted to teaching school weekdays and worship on Sundays. As the Methodist church became more aggressive the membership dropped and the house soon was used solely for a school. When the state made different provisions for smaller districts and new buildings this building was abandoned.

At this point, according to legend, an old negro, "Josh" Clark, moved in and made it his home. He slept on a bed of straw in front of the pulpit. Josh lived there for some years until his death. The building was then torn down and nothing remains now to mark the site.

SARDIS METHODIST CHURCH
with MS. EMMA HARRINGTON
Courtesy of Ms. Louise Kirby

SARDIS METHODIST CHURCH
this years after a face lift
Taken by Roland Beebe

SARDIS METHODIST CHURCH

Religion was a very important part of daily life to the inhabitants of the area. Even before they had a church a society of Methodists was formed and the people met for a religious worship at the homes of the members. Although the population was sparse and the people were weak financially their religious fever and zeal was strong. Among the converts was John Wood, a man of influence and wealth, whose generosity made the first church possible. He not only deeded the land to them but contributed largely to the building fund.

The deed states: "Deed from John Wood and wife to Nathaniel Luff, James Hendrickson, Thomas Sipple, John Parsons, Isaac Jester, John Taylor, Thomas Smith, and James Bell - Trustees for the use, benefit and behalf of the Society of People called Methodists to build a church or preaching house thereon to be occupied and used by such Preachers as are legally authorized to preach the Gospel by the Bishops of the Methodist Episcopal Church in America ....used as a School House by the said Trustees and others for such Schoolmaster....to teach School therein..." Extracted from a Deed in the Officer of the Recorder of Deeds in Kent County in Book D, Vol 2, Page 170: 171.

The first church was a modest undertaking with the dimensions being 20x26 ft on the ground floor, 1 1/2 stories high, with end and side galleries and a seating capacity of 150 persons. This continued as their place of worship for the next fifty-two years until such time as the congregation out grew the church. It was named Sardis in the honor of one of the seven churches of Asia.

During the years there were many preachers who dispensed the gospel from its pulpit. Included in this group was the Reverends Freeborn Garreston, Billy Barnes, Joshua Humphries and William Urie.

The old church had outlived its usefulness and it was necessary to build a new one but the people at that time did not think themselves equal to the task financially, their original benefactor having passed away more than twenty years earlier. The winter of 1841-42 was one of unusual severity with large quantities of snow and ice filling the valleys of the Delaware and Schuylkill rivers. A deluge of rain and the January thaw caused these rivers to overflow their banks and the raging waters carried everything before it. Millyards and lumber wharfs were stripped of their contents and thousands of feet of valuable building material found its way to the bay. The prevailing winds drove it ashore along the beaches of Milford Neck and the people turned out en masse to save as much as possible. Some was returned to its rightful owners, but thousands of feet remained unclaimed.

At this point the proposition to build a new church was revived and a building committee was organized immediately. The committee consisted of Elias Primrose, Benjamin P. Needles, John C. Webb, James Davis, and John Thompson, men representative of the community.

In the years mentioned my property which borders the church, was owned by Levis (Lewis) Passmore of Philadelphia County in Pennsylvania. He deeded over two acres to Elias Primrose, Zadoc Postles, John Webb, Benjamin Needles and James Davis, Trustees of Sardis Meeting House in Milford Neck for the purpose of a house of worship. This piece of property was approximately sixty feet east of the site of the original church.

Though there was plenty of lumber the people still needed money to complete the project. John Thompson, the only member of the board who was not a member of the church, proved to be the most efficient member of the building committee. He was a born diplomat and knew precisely how to approach wealthy men of other communities and obtain liberal donations.

The foundation was laid and by the latter half of 1842 the superstructure was begun. This building was 26x30 feet, 18 1/2 feet high with side and end galleries and would seat an audience of 250 people. The galleries were similar to those at Barratt's Chapel. At the time of construction it was considered one of the counties most important country churches. The pulpit was elevated about 3 1/2 feet so the speaker could see and be seen by the whole audience. In June, 1843 the church was dedicated to the service of Almighty God. The dedication sermon was preached by Rev. Henry White of the Dover District. He was a descendent of Judge Thomas White who defended Coke and Asbury from the rabble and sheltered them in the gloomy days of Methodism.

The old church was not torn down but used for a time, with the permission of the trustees, by the negroes as a place to hold clap and prayer meetings. In 1848 or 1849 the negroes no longer were using it so it was used as a School House for the accommodation of the citizens of the community until a District School house was built. The building, by then in a dilapidated condition, was sold to Nathanial Luff for $30, whereupon he moved it to his nearby property.

The first minister to occupy the pulpit after dedication was the Rev. William Connelly of the Milford Circuit. Under the preaching of Rev. Connelly a powerful revival was realized and scores were added to the membership of the church. Old fashioned tallow candles were used to light the evening services.

The years of 1844-1845 brought Pastor William Quinn and junior preacher Charles Schock and in 1846-1847 Rev. James L. Houston was minister with Rev. Andrew Manship as associate. Rev. Manship was a young man and one of the greatest Evangelists this peninsula has ever produced. He was a powerful motivator and intensely zealous and conducted some of the greatest revivals in the history of this church. Following these were Rev. William C. Flannery for two years, Rev. Elon J. Way for two years, and Rev. Joseph B. Aspril. Rev. Aspril's associate Samuel T. Gardner was by far the abler man, who possessed much talent, ability and great power. These two were the last to serve while the church was attached to the Milford Circuit. The minister under Rev. Aspril in 1850 was Rev. Thomas Jefferson Quigley, PE and below is a list of the church members at that time:

John Webb.....Sarah Webb.....Mary Needles
John Livingston.....Mary Thompson.....William Needles
Amelia Livingston.....Margaret Hall.....Sarah Cullen
Elizabeth Cullen.....Clarisa Thomas.....Nancy Powell
Elizabeth Welch.....John Needles.....Mary Davis
Sarah Thompson.....James Davis.....Sarah Davis
Elizabeth Bowman.....Mary Jester.....Mitchell Webb
Rachel C. Webb.....Sylvester Webb.....Mary Webb
John Maloney.....Mary Maloney.....Robert Watkins
Isaac Jester.....Elizabeth Jester.....Nancy Watkins
Ann Jester.....Nathaniel Thomas.....Sarah Meradith
Elizabeth Thomas.....Matthew Mitten.....Mary Mitten

Shadrach Postles.....Cynthia Postles.....Noah Fowler
Phoebe Fowler.....Noah Wheatly.....Sarah Watson
Daniel Mitten.....Brinkley Mitten.....Sarah Mitten
James H. Postles.....Rachel C. Jester.....James Walker
Catherine Walker.....Sarah Masten.....Sarah Coverdale
Samuel Thompson.....Rachel Thompson.....Giden Willey
Sarah Holleger.....Cathering Holleger.....Henry Bradley
Mary Masten.....Sealy Ann Wadkins.....William Suthel
Benjamin Ennis.....Robert H. Hollis.....Mary Maginnis

In 1855 the church was a part of the circuit with Frederica and Barrett's Chapel and was assigned Rev. J.B. Merritt, one of the ablest ministers in the Philadelphia Conference, for the next two years.

In 1858, in conjunction with Laws and Williamsville Churches, the church was placed with the Harrington Circuit. The church was served by pastor Rev. William B. Walton with whom the people were well satisfied. Following him was Rev. Joseph E. Smith, 1860-1861, a man noted for piety and a powerful pulpit orator. This was during the dark days of the Civil War. On Sunday, July 1, 1861, the day of the beginning of the Battle of Manasses Junction, he preached, to the displeasure of the sympathizers of the Rebellion in his audience, a most powerful and convincing Union sermon. The next pastor was Rev. Henry Sanderson followed by Rev. Arthur W. Milby. Right after Rev. Milby was probably one of the greatest orators, due to his style and marvelous eloquence, this peninsula ever produced. He went on from here to become a well-known and respected pastor throughout the country and even served in the Congress of the United States for a time. I am speaking of the Rev. Jonathan S. Willis whose many friends felt he was a gifted man and always there to help when needed. It was about this time, 1867-1868, the Philadelphia Conference was divided and the Wilmington Conference created. The pastor which followed Rev. Willis was the Rev. A. D. Davis. He was a zealous active worker and accomplished much good during his three year stay. In the year 1873 the church was in a healthy condition both spiritually and financially. It was decided to add an addition of 18 feet to the length and entirely remodel the building. This was done by removing the galleries and laying a floor to the second story, thereby making it an auditorium. The work was completed by June, 1874, at a cost of $1100.00, and a rededication sermon was preached by Rev. James B. Mann. Every dollar necessary to meet the obligation was raised through the determined energy and untiring efforts of the committee consisting of Joshua Bennett, George Thomas, Jehu Davis, John P. Needles, and David K. Watson. Though the efforts of the women of the church, furnishings such as carpets and other necessities were obtained.

The first organ installed in the church was during the pastorate of Rev. R.K. Stevenson, who later was Superintendent of the Dover District. And the first music played for an audience was by his wife.

The handsome bible that graces the ministerial desk was a gift of Nathanial P. Luff in memory of his mother who had been a consistent and exemplary member.

For eight years the church was associated with Barrett's Chapel. Then for a period of two years it was made a station with Isaiah T. Johnson as pastor the first year and Rev. Wilmar Jaggard the second. The church was then put back on the Houston Circuit with F.C. McSorley as pastor. The next thirteen years brought many pastors. Included during the years of 1911 and 1912 was the Rev. C.B. Kitchen Below is a program from the Temperance Day of 1911.

Singing............................National Hymn

Prayer, by the pastor...............Rev. C.B. Kitchen

Responsive Reading.................."What the Bible Says"

Recitation, "The Drink Evil".........H.A. Thompson

Hymn................................Rescue the Perishing

Declamation..........................Bishop Fowler

Arraignment..........................Miss Lulu Kirby

Recitation...........................Miss Sarah V. Thompson

Declamation, Gov. Hauley's Climax....Miss Volita Maloney

Reading, "Some Startling Facts about the Drink Traffic"

Closing Hymn........................."God Bless Our Cause"

Also during that period Rev. C.M.Levister, D.D. of the Baltimore Conference, Editor of the Methodist, the official organ of the Baltimore and Wilmington Conferences, filled the pulpit of Milford Neck Church on Sunday afternoon, June 25, 1911, preaching a very able sermon on "Love to Jesus Christ." The Ladies of the Aid Society during this time of year held ice cream and strawberry festivals in the grove by the church to which the public was invited.

The next pastor following the thirteen year period was Rev. W.E. Thompkinson who was laboring under a sad mental affliction that utterly incapacitated him from work. When he was sent to serve for a second year there was great dissatisfaction and a strong protest. Two appointments on the charge withdrew and at the request of Rev. T.A.H. Obrien were added to his charge, Frederica.

In September of 1921 it was decided to incorporate the church. The Certificate of Incorporation of Milford Neck Methodist Episcopal Church listed the duly elected trustees as Joseph C. Bennett, Samuel C. Thompson, Frisby Kirby, William E. Maloney, Alfred M. Meredith, George H. Jester and Harvey Thompson. In 1930 the Board of Trustees voted to give the ground between the present church and the first church to the state to facilitate putting in a public road to South Bowers.

A small edition was added in 1933 for a kitchen and to accommodate a 750 watt automatic Delco plant to provide electric lights in the church. The church had as its pastor from 1926-1936 the Rev. N.C. Benson. The pastor in 1936 was Rev. Hugh Kelso and the Board of Trustees consisted of Harvey A. Thompson, Harvey Clifton, Paris Kirby, Iva Sharp and J. Raymond Bennett.

In the latter part of 1943, when Rev. David E. Wood was pastor, this area suffered a violent wind storm which caused extensive damage to the church from an uprooted tree. Repairs were made and services were uninterrupted. In the mid fifties the Board elected as Chairman Harvey A. Thompson, Secretary Amanda Short and Treasurer James Webb. All during this time Mrs. Sarah Webb was very active in the church and helped through donations and serving as Superintendent at the Sunday school.

In 1960 the pastor was Rev. J. Thomas Churn who was followed by Rev. George W. Bishop who served a long and loving relationship with the congregation from 1961 to 1971. The next pastor to serve this church was Rev. Gordon Givens from 1972 to 1976. He was missed very much when he left. His replacement was Rev. Nelson B. Benjamin who served from 1977 to 1981. The Board of Trustees in 1978 consisted of James Truiitt, John Thompson, William Maloney Jr., Paynter Reynolds, John French Sr., Elizabeth Ann George, Paris Kirby, Sarah Webb and James Webb. Following Rev. Benjamin in 1982 was Rev. William Downing who served until he was replaced in 1987 by the present pastor Rev. Charles Walter. There was a write up in The Chronicle in October, 1983 reporting the 193rd anniversary of the Sardis Church. It stated the guest speaker would be Dr. Charles Carpenter with solo performances by Loni Wall and Jack Peterman. The services would be conducted by Rev. William Downing.

As can be seen reading through this chapter many people gave a lot of time and energy to keep this church afloat throughout the years. But I believe no one gave more than Mr. Harvey Thompson. I would therefore like to finish with an article furnished to me by my good friend J. Spencer Willis.

MR. HARVEY THOMPSON in front of the
SARDIS METHODIST CHURCH
Courtesy of Mrs. Sarah Webb

The Lords Prayer Illustrated
Written by Harvey A. Thompson

April 5th 1960

Our Father
        By right of Creation
        By bountiful provision
        By gracious adaption

Who Art in Heaven
        The Throne of thy glory
        The portion of thy children
        The temple of thy angels

Hallowed be thy name
        By the thoughts of our hearty
        By the words of our lips
        By the works of our hands

Thy Kingdom come
        Of Providence to defend us
        Of grace to refine us
        Of glory to crown us

Thy Will be done on earth as it is in Heaven
        Toward us without resistance
        By us without compulsion
        Universally without exception
        Eternally without declension

Give us this day or daily bread
        Of necessity for our bodies
        Of eternal life for our souls

And for give our trespasses
        Against the commands of the laws
        Against the grace of the gospel

As we forgive them that trespass against us
        By deforming our character
        By embezzling our property
        By abusing our persons

And lead us not into temptation but deliver us from evil
    Of overwhelming afflictions
    Of worldly enticements
    Of Satans devices
    Of worldly seduction
    Of Sinful affections

For thine is the Kingdom, the power and the glory forever
    Thy Kingdom governs all
    Thy Power Subdues all
    Thy Glory is above all

Amen
    As it is in thy promises
    So be it in our prayers
    So it shall be in thy Praises

JOHN WESLEY A.M.E. CHURCH
Courtesy of Ms. Constance Bessellieu

INTERIOR OF JOHN WESLEY A.M.E. CHURCH
Courtesy of Ms. Constance Bessellieu

JOHN WESLEY AME CHURCH

I was unable to locate very much in the way of records pertaining to the history of the John Wesley AME Church. It was fortunate that I was able to obtain a history that Ms. Constance Bessellieu compiled for the 141st anniversary of this church. With Ms. Bessellieu's permission this history, a copy of the Homecoming Program of October 19, 1986 and her writings explaining the legend of homecoming are included on the following pages.

HISTORY of JOHN WESLEY AME CHURCH

John Wesley AME Church of Milford, Delaware was founded in September 1845 by a group of dedicated Christians under the leadership of Rev. Peter Loper and Mr. Thomas Mason. The Trustees were: Mr. Nehemiah Scott, Mr. Daniel Garison Scott, Mr. Smart Townsend, Mr. David Davis and Mr. Robert Murphy. The Steward was: Mr. Dennis Cannon. John Wesley AME Church was a member of the Philadelphia annual conference in Philadelphia, PA, the Wilmington District and the East Frederica, Delaware circuit. The Presiding Elder in charge was Elder J.B. Stansbery, DD. The Church was later rebuilt in October 1883. (This information was obtained from a page of a Bible which was presented to the Church on October 15th 1899 by the Deacons). On November 6, 1897 a formal deed was issued to the Trustees of John Wesley AME Church which shows the transfer of property from Mr. and Mrs. Paris Carlisle to the Trustees. The original deed is on file at the office of the Recorder of Deeds in Dover, DE. A corner stone was laid in 1927 while Rev. Morris Harmon served as Pastor. One hundred and forty one years have passed since the founding of the "Little Wooden Church on the Hill" which John Wesley AME Church is fondly called. During this time the Church has been blessed with the very fine Christian leadership of many Bishops, Presiding Elders, Pastors and loyal members. At the present time Bishop Frank Cummings is the Presiding Bishop, Presiding Elder Joseph D. Tull is the Presiding Elder, and Reverend Ethelbert L. Maddox is the Pastor. There are 29 participating members, lots of friends and loyal supporters. John Wesley AME Church is a part of the Dover District of the Delaware Conference under the Delaware Conference of the 1st Episcopal District of the General AME Conference. The Trustees are: Mr. Thurman Games. Mrs. Laura Clark, Mr. Walter Clark, Mr. Owen Deputy and Mrs. Ethel Clark. The Stewards are: Mr. Chester Scott, Mrs. Anna Mosley, Ms. Constance Bessellieu, Mr. Daniel Coleman and Mr. Alex Benson. Other active organizations are: Ladies Aid, Stewardess Board, Ushers Board, Missionary Society, Choir and the Sunday School. Traditionally special services are held to celebrate the anniversary of the John Wesley AME Church on the last Sunday in July each year. John Wesley AME Church prays that its spirit of Christian fellowship and devotion will continue for many years to come with "God's Blessings."

Compiled by
Constance Bessellieu
July 1986

HOMECOMING PROGRAM

JOHN WESLEY A.M.E. CHURCH

OCTOBER 19, 1986
3:30 P.M.

PASTOR - E.L. MADDOX

GREETINGS   CONSTANCE BESSELLIEU
                                   MISTRESS OF CEREMONIES
CALL TO WORSHIP
OPENING HYMN   CENTRAL BAPTIST CHOIR
PRAYER   MRS. EVELYN MOSLEY
SCRIPTURE   MRS. MAEOLA WATSON
SOLO   MR. ALEX BENSON
INTRODUCTION OF SPEAKER   REV. E.L. MADDOX
SERMONIC HYM   CENTRAL BAPTIST CHOIR
MESSAGE   REV. ROLAND COKER, PASTOR
                                   CENTRAL BAPTIST CHURCH
INVITATION   REV. COKER AND REV. MADDOX
OFFERING   MR. DANIEL COLEMAN
                                   MRS. DELORES ELLIOTT
SOLO   MRS. LAVERNE MADDOX
REMARKS   VISITORS, SPONSOR AND
                                   REV. E.L. MADDOX
BENEDICTION   REV. E.L. MADDOX

GIVE US THIS DAY THY WORD
THAT WE MAY LIVE BY MORE
THAN BREAD ALONE.

THE LEGEND OF HOMECOMING AT

JOHN WESLEY A.M.E. CHURCH

This year of 1987, we celebrate the Bi-Centennial year of the AME Church and give honor to the founders, Bishop Richard Allen and his associates. They passed on the feeling of Christian fellowship to many of the early leaders of John Wesley AME Church.

The founders of John Wesley AME Church then passed on the legacy of love and dedication to all of those who followed. Two of those who were inspired by their Christian leadership were Brother Clarence Mosley and Sister Mary E. Draine.

For many years, Brother Clarence Mosley was the self appointed caretaker of the John Wesley AME Church cemetery. He would walk many miles with a bramble scythe and sickle to confront the bees, snakes and briars in order to make the cemetery one of which we could be proud.

The church family felt that Brother Mosley should be compensated for his Christian labor of love. Under the leadership of Sister Mary E. Draine the concept of Homecoming was made a reality when the first Homecoming service was held the 3rd Sunday of October, 1956, to reward Brother Mosley. Many families of members, friends and those who had loved ones buried in the cemetery were contacted. The proceeds were given to Brother Mosley to show our appreciation for the services which he had voluntarily given. From these early proceeds, Brother Mosley was able to purchase a lawn mower and various members provided transportation to ease the hardships he had encountered. Brother Mosley continued his services in this area for as long as his health permitted.

Sister Draine continued the sponsorship of Homecoming through the years until her demise in November 1978. Homecoming was a very exciting time for her and she inspired the church family and friends to the point where we could do other things for the church in addition to the maintenance of the cemetery.

The John Wesley AME Church family so loved the concept of Homecoming the tradition has continued.

We truly pray that this fine tradition may continue for many years to come and that someday there may be a Bi-Centennial Homecoming at out "Little Wooden Church on the Hill."

Compiled by:
Constance Mosley Bessellieu
October 1987

Pastor :
Rev. Ethelbert Maddox
John Wesley AME Church
Milford, Delaware

MY HOME IN 1990
Taken by Roland Beebe

THE HISTORY OF MY HOME

As I said in my introduction the project that started this whole book was to trace the ownership of my property and try to determine the history of my home.

By going through the deeds and wills at the state offices I was able to trace the property back to a grant on December 21, 1680 to Richard Williams of 600 acres which he called "William's Choice." This tract contained my property and was sold by Richard Williams to John Townsend on July 18, 1686 who in turn sold 300 acres of the tract to Samson & Sarah Allen. After Samson Allen died his widow sold the 300 acres to Luke Manlove on November 12, 1701. Luke left it in his will to his son, George Manlove in December of 1708.

After the tract was split out in smaller sections the list of owners became very large and I still could not find anything that showed where anyone had built on my property. This area at that time was called the "Forest" due to the fact that is was all wooded and not very populated.

The first person to build on my property was, to the best of my knowledge, a Lewis Passmore who owned this acreage in the early 1800's. The house was a small one room down and one room up building approximately 20 x 20 feet. The next resident was Nathanal Livingston in 1847. There was a four acre plot that Mr. Livingston sold to Manlove Cole of April 3, 1848. Between April of 1848 and September of 1860 this plot belonged to George Fowler and then Absolom Hill who sold it to Rufs Cannon and then bought it back from Rufs six months later. The balance of the property of sixteen acres, + or - as the deed states, is still intact.

This sixteen acres was sold by Mr. Livingston on September 6, 1851 to George & Elizabeth Fowler who then sold it to Isaac R. Jester on February 17, 1860. Isaac R. Jester lived here all during the Civil War until he sold it on November 27, 1865 to Absolom Hill. Mr. Hill built a store across the street from the house and ran it until his death in 1888, at which time his widow Rachel D. and son George received the property through his will in March on 1888. Daniel A. Thompson purchased the property on September 19, 1888 from the heirs of Absolom Hill. The tract stayed in the Thompson family for many years passing from Daniel on his death to Lydia and then to the children Harvey and Sarah and finally on December 6, 1919 Sarah sold her portion of the property to Harvey Thompson including the store which was still in operation.

OUR BOTTLE COLLECTION
The four clear ones in the center are the Milford and Milton bottles
Taken by Roland Beebe

THE OLD OAK ICEBOX
Taken by Roland Beebe

At some point in time one of the owners built a two story house just to the left and in front of the original house, using the small house as a kitchen. The two story house had two rooms down and four small bedrooms upstairs. On June 5, 1963 Ernest Macklin bought the property at an auction for Wilson C. and Beatrice E. Marvel who used it generally as a summer home. Sometime during the previous years the two story house and the small house had been made into one dwelling. The Macklin's did some remodeling by taking out two partitions upstairs and making it into two bedrooms, adding a kitchen and bath downstairs and a bath upstairs. My wife Ila and I purchased the property on August 29, 1971.

After we were here a while the children found a dumping area in the woods behind the house. My son, Glenn, was able to find bushels of old jars. A number of these were medicine jars from places such as Brooklyn, Ny; Chicago; Camden, NJ;Woodbury, NJ; Georgetown, Mass; Binghamton, NY and Philadelphia. The more interesting ones were the local companies such as Dr. Pratt's Drug Store, Milford, De.; Thos. H. Douglas, Pharmacist, Milton, Del; T. F. Hammersely, Druggist, Milford, Del & L.D. Caulk Company, Milford, De. Many of these bottles we have used as decorations in our home as well as an old oak icebox made by "SUPERB" which we found in a shed out back and refinished for use in the foyer.

THOMPSON STORE (Original Site)
Courtesy of Mrs. Sarah Webb

THOMPSON STORE (Present Site in Lewes)
Taken by Roland Beebe

THE THOMPSON STORE & FAMILY

The Thompson country store was located in Thompsonville which is approximately five miles northeast of Milford. It set directly across from my home which is at the junction of County Roads 19A and 122.

The store is said to have been built in the 1860's by Absolom Hill, who was born in 1825 in Cedar Creek hundred, Sussex County to Absolom and Cassy Hill. Mr. Hill purchased a tract of land from William and Rachel Gray in Milford Hundred in February of 1850. After building a house, outbuildings and otherwise improving the property, he moved in with his new wife Rachel D. Jester. Her parents were Major and Sara Jester also from Cedar Creek Hundred and neighbors to the Hill Family. The census of 1860 shows Absolom and Rachel Hill with three children, George age 7, Sarah E. age 4, and Sarah J. age 4 mos. In the year 1860 Absolom Hill purchased the farm of Isaac R. Jester, which is now my residence, and after a few years moved from the old farm to his new acquisition. We believe it was at this time that he built what we now know as the Thompson Store, which he ran until his death in 1888.

The store had sides of handmade clapboard fastened in place by square nails. As you entered the counter was on the left and on the far end of the counter was a glass showcase about 12 to 16 inches high. There was one or two hanging lamps and a wood stove in the middle of the floor with a large sand box, the spit box, nearby. The counter across the back of the store held loose cookies and crackers in boxes with glass lids. Behind the counter on the left were shelves which held various grocery items. Just inside the door was a three cornered shelve which held a stone pitcher and glass. This pitcher was kept full of water for anyone wanting a drink, and everyone used the same glass. The back room was where the barrels of vinegar, molasses and kerosene were kept. Up a narrow hallway was a tiny storeroom and on close inspection you could see the front wall was plastered. It is believed that at one time it was used as sleeping quarters.

After the death of Mr. Hill his heirs sold the store and farm to Daniel A. and Lydia A. Thompson. Daniel, with his wife, ran the store until his death in 1901, at which time his wife took over the reins until 1917 when she passed on. The post office for the Thompsonville area was in this store at one time. Postmaster General John Wanamaker signed the certificate in 1891 naming Lydia Thompson postmistress of the Thompsonville Post Office, which she ran until the last mail day of March, 1902 at which time Rural Free delivery was started by the federal government. Her children Harvey and Sarah took over, after her death, for a period but Harvey ended up with sole ownership in December, 1919. Mr. Harvey, as he was fondly called, operated the store until July, 1962 at which time, at the age of 87, he retired and closed it. "Don't say that I'm old and decrepit," he said to reporters, with a wink, "Just say that the whole concept of farming has changed and there's no longer a need for a store like this." With these words he ended a long career and in October, 1962 donated the store to the Lewes Historical Society.

The Thompson country store and post office are on display and opened to the public, in the summer months, at the historical complex on the corner of Third and Ship Carpenter Streets in Lewes, Delaware. This store may be the last of the country stores that years ago were found throughout Kent and Sussex Counties.

The Thompson Family

James Thompson, who tenanted the "Big Stone" farm owned by John Steward, later moved to the old "Potter Farm" in the northern part of Milford Neck. The descendants of James eventually ran the Thompson Store. Daniel Thompson was the third child of six born to James and Sarah (Powell) Thompson, his birthday being January 9, 1840. His first marriage was to Mary E. M. Jester on January 14, 1869 and produced a daughter, Mary E. Thompson, on December 1, 1869. He lost his wife on December 17, 1869 and his daughter seven months later in July, 1870.

On January 11, 1873 Daniel Thompson married a second time to Lydia Annie Wilson, daughter of Thomas R. and Lydia (Houston) Wilson. They had one son, Harvey and one daughter, Sarah V.

At one point Daniel Thompson and George Hill, son of Absolom Hill, went in partnership. They ran a saw mill and cannery which was located about 100 yards Southwest of the Sardis Church on the land of Absolom Hill. They were built by Hiram Barber in 1882, the mill being finished in March and the cannery later that same year.

The Milford Chronicle of Friday, October 26, 1883 reads:

Thompson & Hill Cannery
Have sold one-third of pack. Tomatoes 93,000 cans
Paid $6.00 per ton for tomatoes. Grapes a few cans
Yield in this neighborhood below average.

The Polk Directory of 1884 - Milford listed:
Thompson & Hill, saw mill, fruit pack and general store
8 miles NE.

After the death of Absolom Hill in 1888, Daniel Thompson acquired complete ownership of these ventures through purchasing all the business and farm from the heirs. He went on to operate the mill and store until his death.

During this period Harvey, his son, went to Goldey College and graduated in 1897. As a student his parents gave him $3.00 and $3.50 on alternate weeks for living expenses. The extra $.50 every other week was for laundry. In 1898 he returned home and taught school in one of the country schools in the area. He decided to go out on his own in 1899, at which time he worked as a clerk for the A&P in Philadelphia for $6.00 a week and paid $4.00 a week board.

MR. HARVEY HIS PRIZE PIGS
Courtesy of Mrs. Sarah Webb

It did not take long for him to see he was getting nowhere fast. He decided to move back home and from 1901 to 1924 he was owner and operator of the mill as well as working in the store. He also did some farming, which he continued until 1949. Mr. Harvey raised pigs and there was an unwritten contest to see who could raise the largest hogs in Milford Neck and Mr. Harvey's were generally the biggest around.

He was a church leader all his life, being a member of the board and superintendent of the Sardis Methodist Church. He also served as a member of the advisory board of the Delaware Trust Company, Frederica Branch for many years. On his retirement in 1962 he told reporters, "There were no paved roads when I started...all dirt roads...except in winter when they froze and spring when they were mud."

Mr. Harvey married Elizabeth Stevenson, daughter of David C. and Amanda J. (Minner) Stevenson, on December 17, 1907 and they were together until her death in March, 1949. They had no children. The stories say that when Mr. Harvey and Mrs. Liza went away for 1/2 day every week they got Buster Jester, or on occasion Spence Willis, to watch the store till closing. They were always back by closing. Mr. Harvey had his ways about him and I have been told that in the evening, when the farmers and hunters gathered to discuss the events of the day in the store, he would stretch out on the counter, head on the candy showcase, and read the paper. Also when closing time came Mr. Harvey would get up, wind the big clock and close the shutters. This was your invitation to go home. They say in 1916 he installed a phone in his home and in 1926 he put in a 32 volt electric generator, which he used until he went on REA in 1948. He lived his last years with his sister Sadie Patterson in Milford. Mr. Harvey, affectionately called "The Elder Statesman of Thompsonville" passed away, at the age of 93, in July, 1968.

BENNETT'S PIER

Bennett's Pier, once called Steamboat Landing, was used in the early 1850's as a stop for a steamboat going from Philadelphia to Lewes. This enabled the farmers to ship their crops to the city and receive goods to help with their daily life. According to tavern license records, Joshua Bennett had a hotel and tavern, which was built in 1852, on this site. I am sure this was for the convenience of the passengers which also made the trip. There was a tremendous high tide on Sunday, April 19, 1854 which completely inundated the marshes and low lands and in the process flooded the hotel with water as deep as twelve inches. Also on Pier Beach were some fishing shanties and although privately owned they were always open to the public. I have been told that some of the shanties were used for family picnics, family reunions and by fisherman as late as the 1940's. The only requirement was that it was left as you found it, which meant cleaned and the dishes and pans washed and put away.

The steamboat that was on this line from 1851 until the fall of 1855 was the St. Nicholas. Based on information I received from a number of sources the St. Nicholas that was purchased for this line was probably the one built in Brooklyn, New York in 1845. This boat was a sidewheeler weighing 413 tons and its first port was New York, New York. The Captain of the vessel in June of 1853 was Enos Whitaker and the St. Nicholas would leave from Philadelphia every Monday, Wednesday and Friday mornings at 7 a.m. stopping at Newcastle, Mahon's River and Bennett's Pier and make return trips leaving from Lewes every Tuesday, Thursday and Saturday mornings at 7 a.m. stopping at the same places. Stages connected with the boat at Lewes from Cherry Stone, VA via Drummontown, Horntown, Snow Hill, Berlin and Millsboro, also from Princess Anne via Salisbury, Laurel and Georgetown. At Bennett's Pier the stage from Canterbury, Frederica and Milford would meet the boat and at Mahon's River there was a stage from Dover. The fare for riding the boat was $2.00 from Philadelphia to Lewes, $1.75 from Mahon's River to Lewes and $1.25 from Bennett's Pier to Lewes.

It is interesting to note that once the steamer "St. Nicholas" left this area she made a regular scheduled run between Baltimore and Georgetown, D.C. on the Potomac River. On June 28, 1861 she was boarded at various points by Confederates posing as passengers. The leaders of the group Col. R. Thomas, CSA and Capt. G.N. Hollins, CSN, with their men seized the steamer near Point Outlook. Captain Hollins took command and headed the ship down to the Chesapeake Bay, where she took three prizes on June 29th. The "St. Nicholas" was condemned as a prize and the Confederate Navy put the command in the hands of Lt. H. H. Lewis, CSN and he operated in the Potomac and Rappahannock until April of 1862 when she was burned by the Confederates at Fredericksburg, VA., to keep the Union from taking possession of her.

THE BENNETT'S
Back Row L to R: Elizabeth, Ida, William & George
Front Row L. to R: Janie, John, Joe, Joshua & Annie
Courtesy of Mrs. Sarah Webb

OLD FISHING SHANTIES ON PIER BEACH
Courtesy of Mr. & Mrs. Spence Willis, Jr.

PRESENT HOME OF TOM WEBB
Taken by Roland Beebe

THE BENNETT'S

Joshua Bennettt reared a family of nine children who were said to have great longevity because they were all past seventy before the first one died. George Bennett was a blacksmith, Joe was a farmer who, after retirement, lived in the house on the corner opposite the church, and Johnny lived in the first house on the left past the church on the road to South Bowers. Albert Webb told me "The house where Tom Webb now lives was originally part of the hotel that was on Pier Beach. It was moved up to its present site by Joshua Bennettt and made into a home. It is only a one and a half story house because when workmen were trying to remove wasp nests from under the eaves the second story was accidentally burned off.

THE WEBB'S

John Wesley Collins Webb lost his parents before he was sixteen and he was bound to his uncle, Alexander Argo. Before the expiration of his indenture he was placed on the farm of his uncle's sister, Margaret Webb, where he managed the entire property for a one-third share of the crops. After two years he had saved enough to buy some hogs and a pair of oxen to start farming for himself. He leased the Postles farm and then the Townsend farm where he spent seven years. He then leased land from Daniel Goodwin for five years. According to the Byles Map III, Kent, 1859 J.W.C. Webb owned over 200 acres near Webbs Landing. One of his children, Francis Albert married Mary L. Bennett and their son Francis Albert II was married to Sarah Sipple who was born to James and Jennie (Maloney) Sipple in December of 1891. Due to the death of Sarah's mother, when she was only three, Sarah was raised by her namesake, Grandmother Sarah Sipple, along with her sister Naomi.

WEBB FAMILY
L to R: Bill, Allie, Sarah, Tom, Albert & James
Courtesy of Mrs. Sarah Webb

This was because Grandmother Sipple lived closer to the school and perhaps because her father took another wife. They were educated at the local school until they were transferred to the Frederica school. In 1908 when Mr. Harvey Thompson drove by horse and buggy to pick up the doctor from Frederica for Grandmother Sipple he also picked up Sarah from school and brought her home. Her education ended at this point and she nursed her grandmother until her death in 1911. That same year there was a typhoid epidemic in the community which she and her sister both contracted. Sarah was able to survive her sickness but lost her sister, Naomi. The one positive thing that happened to her that year was her marriage, which took place in late July, to Francis Albert Webb III. "Allie", as everyone called him, and Sarah had four sons named James, Albert, William and Thomas. Sarah was very active in the Sardis Church, serving as superintendent of the Sunday School for close to fifty years. She was chaplin of the Captain Jonathan Caddwell Chapter of the DAR for many years and spent over twenty years working with the American Red Cross. She was also an active Grange member and chaplin for the Founders and Patrons of Delaware. Mrs. Sarah E. Webb is one of four women in Milford listed in the book "Delaware Women Remembered." Allie was at one time employed as a milk tester for the Sussex County Dairy Herd Improvement Association and as one of his duties he would go around the county checking the butterfat content of milk at dairy farms. Sarah's husband, Allie, passed away in 1956. In 1973 her son Bill died of a heart attack while answering a fire alarm. The family farm is carried on by Tom, his son Tom (Tubby) and Bill's son Skip. To update Sarah's other two sons; Albert, with his wife Sarah, lives near Houston, DE and James, retired from J. C. Penny, lives in Thompsonville with his wife Theresa.

Mrs. Sarah E. Webb, a grand lady and neighbor, passed away October 27, 1985. She is missed by everyone in the community who knew and loved her.

SOUTH BOWERS

South Bowers was started basically as a summer getaway. This beautiful summer resort is divided from North Bowers Beach by the Murderkill River and in those times its inviting appearance, for those wishing to spend an outing, or a fortnight, or even the whole season, caused it to progress as a resort. While some of the cottages were built for the purpose of renting to visitors there were a number built and furnished as a summer residence at a considerable cost and were occupied by their owners. A few of the cottages were owned by doctors and lawyers from Philadelphia.

Most of the cottages were given names such as "Mount Airy" which was owned by Mrs. George Blanchard of Frederica. "Milford Gables" was owned by Mr. Charles Barker who said he derived pleasure from the fishing, clamming and bathing. "Bee Hive" was owned by Mr. Oscar Bie, a ship chandler from Philadelphia. "Midnight Sun" was owned by one of the pioneers in cottage building on the south side, Mr. Kirts of Woodbury, N.J. The property of Mr. and Mrs. Walter Daniels was simply known as "Daniels." George A. Hincken, of Philadelphia, had perhaps the largest and most costly cottage on the shore and called it "Hincken." "Point Comfort" the cottage of Mrs. L. A. Thompson was always active with Miss Sadie entertaining friends, relatives and on occasion her Sunday School class. "Chermire" was occupied by Dr. Clawson Beswick, of Philadelphia, a leading force in the organizing of a fire company. "Riverside" Store belonged to Mr. & Mrs. Irvin Scott. "Bayview" Hotel which was so popular the proprietor had to secure a large cottage on occasion to handle the overflow.

The steamboat "Frederica" stopped at North Bowers and this is how they traveled from Philadelphia to their cottages. The only way from North to South Bowers, although it was only a few yards across the Murderkill river, was a large rowboat owned by Dave Mills, who charged five cents a head to transport people across the creek. The only other way was to take a horse and buggy and ride out to the highway, through Frederica, down the Thompsonville road and on into South Bowers which was approximately fifteen miles.

In early years, as well as now, the area has been plagued at times by storms and high tides. An example of this would be the high tide accompanied by a fearful and devastating storm of October, 1877 known as the "Tidal Wave." According to accounts it came with all the force and fury that waves driven by gale force winds, as high as eighty miles per hour, could inflict. On land and sea the devastation was indescribable. Vessels were swept from their moorings and driven ashore, with many of the smaller craft being carried into corn fields along the mainline. Much of the damage on land included trees being broken off or blown over, houses were unroofed, some homes were completely blown down, large numbers of livestock were injured, and the public highway was rendered impassible due to the debris that was strewn about.

Another storm occurred January 15, 1881 and was known in this section as the "Ice Tide." There was a heavy snow fall and the bay was filled with floating ice, which by the action of the wind, was piled high upon the beach. This formed, for a while, a strong barrier against the incoming water. When the large mass of ice and snow gave away a volume of water and ice, five or six feet in depth, swept over the marshes and low lands carrying everything moveable before it. Fences were carried away and worst of all nearly sixty percent of the livestock was destroyed. It was the custom of the time for farmers who lived on marsh farms and also those who lived nearby to allow all their stock, not needed at home, to remain on the marshes during the winter. Hundreds of cattle were swept before the roaring tide and were strewn for miles on the land when the tide receded. Nearly every farmer along the shore lost a large number of his stock. With the toil of many years being lost it was a very long time before such extensive herds of cattle again roamed over the bay marshes.

ORIGINAL FIRE HALL IN SOUTH BOWERS
Taken by Roland Beebe

PRESENT HOME OF THE SOUTH B OWERS FIRE COMPANY
Taken by Roland Beebe

THE FIRE COMPANY

The driving force behind organizing a fire company in South Bowers Beach was Dr. Clawson Beswick a dentist from Philadelphia. Sometime in the late 1920's Dr. Beswick purchased a Model "T" Ford fire truck from Upper Darby, Pennsylvania. The truck had two seventy five gallon gravity fed tanks. It was driven to South Bowers and for a period of time was kept in a garage until a firehouse was built on land acquired from Sarah E. Webb in July, 1931.

The early members of the South Bowers Volunteer Fire Company included:

Preston Brittingham   Dr. Beswick
Lewis Shemire   Dr. Kennick
Casper Powell   Albert Webb, Sr.
Purnell Powell   Samuel Powell

Dr. Beswick, the first president, along with Sam Powell helped finance the building of the first fire house which still stands today. The fire house was built with the labor of its members. It was a two story concrete block structure and is now owned by William and Nancy Finkley.

Samuel Powell ran a grocery store in South Bowers and was one of the first Delaware State Troopers. The State Highway Department established the State Highway Police which was a uniformed force of six men who used motorcycles to perform their duties. These duties consisted of regulating speed, traffic and overloaded trucks.

Sam's son, Purnell Powell, was the fire chief when on Saturday, April 2, 1932 at 3:15 PM a fire swept through South Bowers, jumped the Murderkill River to North Bowers and by the time it was brought under control had destroyed sixteen cottages, two stores and a number of garages and out buildings. It was reported by the Delaware Republican of April 8, 1932 that the fire companies present were: North Bowers, South Bowers, Magnolia, Camden-Wyoming, Milford, Harrington, Felton, Smyrna, Clayton, Townsend, Hartly, and two engines from Dover. They used the Delaware Bay and the Murderkill River which gave them an ample supply of water, but the strong southwest winds fanned the fire and caused embers to fly through the air to surrounding buildings.

Below is a list of properties destroyed and estimated loss according to the Delaware Republican, April 8, 1932.

John George-Frederica,double cottage & contents	4000
Walter Green-Rising Sun, cottage & contents	2000
William Burris-Smyrna,cottage & contents	1500
Postles(recently sold), cottage & contents	2800
Martin Hopewell-Wilm.,2 cottages & contents	5000
Benjamin Detarris-double cottage & contents	6000
John Conner-Smyrna, cottage & contents	3400

John Purnell-Milford,3 cottages & contents	5500
B. Ewing-Bowers, cottage & contents	3000
Sam Powell-S.Bowers,store & dwelling	2500
Preston Brittingham-cottage & contents	3000
Purnell's Store-Bowers, building	500
Warner Green-garage	100

A sub-station was built by the fireman, at Thompsonville, in 1968. The land for the station was acquired by the fire company from one of its members, Clinton Adams, at a nominal fee. The two reasons I was given for having this sub-station was the larger year round population in the Thompsonville area and having the fire hall and equipment more centralized in the district the company was responsible for. The sub-station was enlarged in 1981 and is now, with the sale of the original fire house, the home of the South Bowers Volunteer Fire Company.

THOMPSONVILLE

After much research I have been unable to pinpoint exactly when the name of Thompsonville was first used for this small village. There were many Thompson families in the area and much of the land around and in Thompsonville was owned by either William Thompson, John Thompson, James Thompson or Margaret Thompson, according to deeds recorded in Dover. The Delaware State Directory of 1894-1895 contained the following article:

>An agricultural village eight miles from Milford, its
>nearest railroad station, and six miles from Frederica.
>Three miles from Delaware Bay. In 1894 land valued at
>$50 per acre. Principal products corn, wheat, tomatoes,
>and potatoes. M.E. Church and two public schools convenient.

George W. Jester, Wheelwright
Alexander Kirby, mail carrier
D. A. Thompson, merchant
James H. Webb, Jr., postmaster
Schuyler Kirby & Edward Short, fishermen

Farmers

John W. Adams	William E. Hall
John H. Bennett	Winlock Hall
Joseph C. Bennett	Jacob Harrington
Joshua Bennett, Jr.	Elias Jester
Joshua Bennett, Sr.	Frisby Kirby
John Evans	William Mills
Joseph French	James Sipple
William H. French	Isaac M. Thomas
John R. Wadkins	Daniel Watson
Alfred F. Webb	

The oldest map showing Thompsonville, I have found, was made in the early 1900's. In the History of Delaware, edited by Wilson Lloyd Bevan, Ph.D., during the same period, Thompsonville is listed as: a hamlet of twenty inhabitants about eight miles from Milford. It has one store.

In the late 1920's as you rode down County Road 19 from Route 113 towards South Bowers the first crossroads you came to was Jenkins Crossroads where a fruit drying establishment was on the right. The second crossroads was Herring's Crossroads where, on one corner, set the Herring farm. This farm was also the home of Dorothy Sisson for many years. The next crossroads was Swing Tree Crossroads which is supposed to have gotten its name, many years earlier, from a large swing in a tree on the corner. You then come to Thompsonville, a small village with much history. After passing Thompsonville you would come to Webb's Landing and then to South Bowers Beach which is shown on a map of 1850 as Shurley's Bar. The road going from Route 113 to Thompsonville was, in 1925, improved from a dirt road to an 18 foot cement road. The road from Frederica to Thompsonville, which was dirt, was resurfaced in the summer of 1932 by being grated, widened and covered with slag.

THE EARLY 1900'S

A ride through the length and breath of Milford Neck in early May, 1911 was a delight, made up of several causes. From Milford to the Tub Mills, which was along the road to Dover, everybody knew of its beauty and attractiveness; but from the time your turn from that main road was made, the real "Turkey Neck," or Milford Neck began and for ten miles to Bennett's Pier, the prosperity of the farmer was apparent in the large flocks of poultry, the sleek cattle and fat horses and mules which were around each home. The crops looked well, but showed the effect of the dry weather which had prevailed. In the past five years, before this, many new homes and great improvements to farm buildings generally had been added, and the general cleanliness about the homes told the story of modern conveniences. At each home large piles of wood cut into lengths for burning in the stoves, was convenient for housewives, showing a realization of the fact that time was spent in chopping wood during the summer. That it was more economical in real cash, to have sawed by traction engine power in the winter, and thus make life more endurable for the women and more comfortable for the men the year around.

There was not much old fashioned clover in the fields of Milford Neck, in comparison with the fields of other seasons; but the wheat looked well although the straw was short. Corn was looking fine, and should a rain fall in the next few days, the pea crop in this neck would be very satisfactory to the growers.

When the drive reached the lower part of Milford Neck, the roads were a dream of excellence; the city was as hard as macadam, and it was a pleasure to ride over them. If the same could be said of them the entire year, it would have been a blessing.

The mosquito crop was numerous of course, you couldn't have all pleasure sailing, but they did not affect the pleasure when the ride was made in an automobile. Milford Neck looks fine in the spring.

The preceding article appeared in the MILFORD CHRONICLE dated MAY 26, 1911.

Many tales are told about incidents that took place in Milford Neck. One such incident concerns the wife of a prominent farmer by the name of Samuel E. Bickel. In the spring of 1912 Mr. Bickel's wife decided to start a little enterprise of her own. Because she used so much raw cotton for domestic purposes, and the price had increased so much, she secured the seed cotton, had her husband direct some men to prepare the ground and she saw that the cotton seed was properly planted. The venture turned out to be very successful and she had all the raw cotton she needed that fall.

The Christmas holidays always brought the business season to a close, except for the last two weeks before Christmas and the week after when the good people of this section were very much occupied. They had to manufacture and ship holly and greens for decorations, not to mention the great shipments of some of the finest turkeys, geese, ducks and chickens which were dressed and shipped from Milford Neck to Philadelphia. Probably one hundred tons, of all kinds, were sent from the neck in that three week period, with the money going into the pockets of the fine women who assisted the farmers of Milford Neck throughout the year. Social enjoyment would commence once the people of the neck were over the Christmas activities mentioned above and there was no people on earth who could better enjoy themselves at parties and church socials than the people of this bit of the land.

MAP of the DELAWARE RIVER

The Clyde of America

The State of Delaware
IX-10

Courtesy of Delaware State Archives

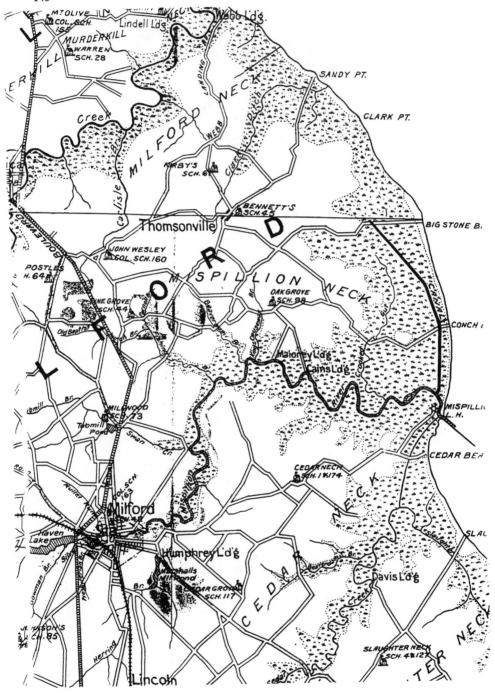

KIRBY'S SCHOOL
Courtesy of Delaware State Archives

CLASS PICTURE: KIRBY'S SCHOOL, YEAR UNKNOWN
Courtesy of Mrs. Sarah Webb

PINE GROVE SCHOOL #44
Courtesy of Delaware State Archives

PINE GROVE SCHOOL CLASS PICTURE
Taken in 1907 or 1908
Courtesy of Mrs. Louise Kirby

BENNETT'S GATE SCHOOL

152

JOHN WESLEY COLORED SCHOOL (Old Building)

JOHN WESLEY COLORED SCHOOL (building of 1921)
Courtesy of Delaware State Archives

EDUCATION

In 1796 the Legislature directed that the funds from the sale of marriage and tavern licenses be set aside in a school fund and allowed the State Treasury to accept gifts, donations, and bequests from individuals for this fund. The school fund was not used until about 1817, at which time the state appropriated $1000 to each county for the education of poor children.

Willard Hall, a lawyer and later judge of the Federal District Court in Delaware, drafted an act establishing free schools and had it passed in the 1829 Legislature. Responsible State control, through the State constitution on 1897, opened the way for uniform taxation for schools and by 1907 compulsory attendance was required by law.

The new School Board of Education, in 1911, included:

Dr. George W. Twitmyer	Wilmington
Henry Ridgley	Dover
George S. Messersmith	Lewes
Professor Harry Hayward	
John W. Hering	Milford
Henry Clay Davis	Laurel
Frederick Brady	Middletown

They were instructed to report on school conditions and suggest revisions of the laws. The first code, later revised, was adopted by the state in 1919-21.

Milford Hundred had a number of community schools according to a map of 1900-1920. The ones in the general area of Thompsonville included:

1) Kirby's
2) Sour Apple Tree
3) Bennett's Gate
4) Pine Grove (School 44)
5) John Wesley - the one colored school

There were annual inspections of the Kent County School Buildings by the School Commission, usually in the spring. The next few excerpts were taken from those school inspections in April of 1911.

Kirby, No. 67, in Milford Neck is taught by Mrs. Clarence Jester and is clean, attractive and in good condition. A new flag pole has been erected during the year just passed.

Bennett's Gate, No. 45, has been taken through a course of through repairs and a large attractive front has been added, which has two porches with substantial steps leading to them. Paint has been used to good order on the exterior and the committee plans to paint the interior this summer. Miss Evans is the teacher and the children look clean, bright and proud of their almost new school house. Well done.

Oak Grove (Sour Apple Tree), No. 98, is in Milford Neck and this school has for years been well to the front for cleanliness and for its good state of repair. But this year it has fallen back. There were several window panes broken out, the floor around the stove needs repairing and the room was not a vision of cleanliness. The condition at this school is considerably behind what they have been or what they should be. The children seemed to not have the usual high interest in the school

154

FORMER WILLIS FARM
Taken by Roland Beebe

WILLIS FAMILY TAKEN ABOUT 1928
L to R: Huldah, Burton, Spencer, William & Jack
Courtesy of Mr. & Mrs. Spencer Willis, Jr.

HOME OF WILLIAM WALLS
Taken by Roland Beebe

WHEAT THRASHING IN THE 1800'S
Courtesy of Ms. Louise Kirby

property. Something needs to be done quickly at this school.

Pine Grove No. 44, under the care of Miss Taylor, the teacher, has excellent sanitary conditions, and the school looks well kept. A new cover should be put about the driven pump.

Teachers at three of the schools for the 1905-1906 school year were Miss Mattie Favinger of Frederica at "Bennett's Gate," Miss Lydia Martin at "Oak Grove," her third year and Mrs. Thomas Abbott was at "Schools 44"

To give you some idea of where these schools were I will try to approximate their location with today roads. Sour Apple Tree was located near Scott's Crossroads on Road 124. Kirby's was located on Road 121 about 1 mile past the Sardis church on the right and set in the woods. Bennett's Gate was on Road 122 about 1/2 mile beyond the church on the right hand side. Pine Grove, known as School 44, is at the intersections of Roads 422 and 425 where Pritchett's Repair Shop is located. The John Wesley School is on Road 120 just east of the John Wesley A.M.E. Church.

Two of these school buildings still exist today. The first is the John Wesley School which has been turned into a home. The other, School 44, is not recognizable as it has been completely remodeled and enlarged and is the residence of Mr. and Mrs. Thomas Pritchett.

The first school bus to run out of this area started in the fall of 1926 and was owned and operated by Mr. Harry Fisher. Mr. Fisher lived in the house where Mrs. Sarah E. Webb last resided. The bus started at his home, went straight out to Rt 113, and into Milford on North Street to the Academy. The bus did not go up any side roads so you had to walk to the main road in order to ride it. If you were in the grade which required you to go into Milford the state paid for your transportation, but if you could go to the local school and preferred to get your education in Milford the family had to pay 10 cents per day per child to ride. The bus, which was homemade, used a Model T Ford chassis on which a carpenter had build a body with benches down each side and a double bench down the middle.

Much of the information on the school bus was furnished by J. Spence Willis, Jr. whose family moved into the area about this time. Spence was born in Lincoln, De., and the family moved to Milford in December of 1919. They resided of Montgomery Street in a house which sat where the Telephone Company now has its office. Spence, Sr. decided to move out of town in 1925 and built a house, now the home of Mr. William Parker, between Herring's Crossroads and Swing Tree Crossroads on the left. The land he purchased included the area where William Walls now lives. This area was used by Spence Willis, Sr. to build a saw mill. Vic Steele, the son-in-law of Senator John Williams, came from Millsboro to run the mill for Mr. Willis. Vic also brought his wheat thrasher with him and used it to pick cow peas throughout Kent County. Cow peas were used during this period of time for feed and fertilizer.

Island Field Site

While building a roadbed across the marshlands just south of South Bowers in 1928 workmen found a large concentration of human bones. Realizing they had uncovered Indian graves they reburied the bones in the immediate vicinity. This was the first time the presence of prehistoric artifacts and remains, which later became the Island Field Site, were known to be in this area. A local farmer and amateur archeologist, Frank Austin, began to surface collect artifacts and acquired a sizeable collection. In 1954, with Mr. Austin's encouragement, the Sussex Society of Archaeology and History made a test excavation. It was 1965 before State Archaeologist Ronald Thomas made a survey of the site and decided it was potentially significant. A full excavation took place in the summer of 1966 and produced, among other things, an adult male burial. On August 7, 1967 the main cemetery was discovered and a temporary shelter was built to provide some protection from the weather.

The State of Delaware authorized funds so that in February of 1969 the purchase of the Island Field Site, approximately 5 acres was made from the F.A. Webb family and the Research Center/Museum building could be constructed. The Museum was completed and opened to the public in 1972.

The Webb Phase people, a designation chosen in honor of the farming Webb family that owned the land, apparently occupied the Delmarva Peninsula about a thousand years ago and were living here about 740 A.D.

This museum has been visited by many groups and families through out the years. The skeletal remains, which were on display until 1988 were ceremoniously reburied after the Nanticoke Indians persuaded the state that this was the proper thing to do. The museum is still opened with the excavation site, burial pits and many exhibits and artifacts on display.

158

COL. WOOD MONUMENT ON CORNER OPPOSITE CHURCH
ERECTED BY SARAH LISTER HALL
FRONT AND BACK
Taken by Roland Beebe

DELAWARE GOVERNORS

There were three governors and one almost governor of Delaware who had a connection with Milford Neck. Below is an account of these governors taken from information at the Hall of Records in Dover.

Henry Molleston III was elected October 5 and died November 11,1819 before he could be inaugurated as governor. Henry, the son of Henry and Sarah (Manlove) Molleston II, was born in Thompsonville about the year 1762. His sister Jemima Ann was married to Colonel John Haslet, whose son Joseph served as Governor of Delaware from 1811 to 1814 and a second term, in which he died in office, in the year 1823.

Although Charles Polk, Governor from 1827 to 1830 and again from 1836 to 1837, was born near Bridgeville in 1788, he acquired 1100 acres near Thompsonville in 1816. After he retired from state politics, at the age of 52, Polk settled on his farm near Bennett's Pier. Charles Polk died October 27, 1857 at the age of 68. The site of his home, which burned in 1929, is two and one half miles Northeast of Thompsonville on County Road 122.

John Wood Hall, Governor from 1879 to 1883, also had a connection with the area. Winlock Hall, born in Milford Neck in the early 1700's, was the grandfather of Governor Hall. Governor Hall's daughter Sarah (Hall) Lister erected a monument in Thompsonville in 1909. It was in memory of the governors namesake, Colonel John Wood and his wife Mary who were early settlers in the area. Mrs. Lister also erected other monuments is the area.

STRATHAM FARM MONUMENT
Taken by Roland Beebe

NEWSPAPER TIDBITS FROM THE PAST

Milford Chronicle

January 12, 1883

The masons are finishing the interior of Mr. D.A. Thompson's new dwelling which will be occupied by Jos. French.

Feb. 23, 1883

Friday, February 16th M.J. Dow of Maine, instituted a Lodge of Good Templars in Milford Neck. It is to be called "Bay View."

Charter officers:

WCT Albert Webb
WVT Jennies Hill
LD James H. Thomas
W Secty Ida R. Bennett
WAS Delia Jester
WFS Will Bennett
ST Lizzie Bennett
WC Laura Mills
WM John Sipple
WDM Lizzie French
WIG Maggie Hall
WOG Joseph Thomas
WRHS Lizzie A. Bennett
WLHS Annie French
PWCT William Mills

They will meet Thursday evenings.

Feb. 5, 1909

Meeting in Thompsonville
There will be a meeting of the farmers at Thompsonville on Monday evening Feb. 8th for the purpose of organizing a Rural Telephone Company for a line from Milford to Webbs Landing.

Jan. 13, 1911

Thompsonville Gun Club (scores)

	Targets	Broke
W.E. Mills	25	18
Joe Bennett	25	14
George Jester	25	15
W. Holleger	25	12
A. Webb, Jr.	25	17
H.A. Thompson	25	11
F.Holleger	25	5
Isaac Jester	10	6
John Bennett	10	3

MILFORD CHRONICLE

April 28, 1911

Concert given by teacher and pupils of John Wesley public school was a success.

May 19, 1911

Trout fish seem to be plentiful at Pier Beach this season. Wilber E. Mills having caught 1400 bushels at one haul last week.

June 30, 1911

James H. Thomas and family will move to their hotel "Bay View" at South Bowers.

Aug 4, 1911

Sunday Aug 6th the famous Berge Sisters, singing evangelists, will arrive at Milford Neck church and sing every evening for two weeks.

May 3, 1912

Trout Fishing at Bennett's Pier

They have been getting large hauls on a regular basis. Their is a boarding house where one can get meals at all times of the day a reasonable rates.

MILFORD CHRONICLE

July 18, 1919

Last Sat. Eve. Albert Webb accompanied by his son reported they believed that Anthrax existed in Milford Neck. Dr. Hiram P. Eves, head of veterinary Dept. of Delaware, came to Milford to verify the claim at the home of H. Webb, on the Sipple Farm, near South Bowers, they found authenticated cases at the home of Mr. Jester, on the Slaughter Farm, they also found Anthrax existing. Webb lost five head and Jester lost two head. The dead cattle have to be burned within 24 hours. Inoculations were began immediately under the supervision of Dr. Evans G. Roberts, a local veterinarian. Before Anthrax was brought under control 13 animals died in Milford Neck with Alfred Webb, Jr. losing the most, which was five.

The **Rescue**...Editor & Proprietor...Rev. A.D. Davis
Devoted to Temperance, Moral Reform and General news

April 3, 1874

GOOD TEMPLAR PLATFORM
Adopted at the Session of the Right Worthy
GRAND LODGE OF 1859

1. Total Abstinence from all intoxicating liquors as a beverage.

2. No license in any form, or under any circumstances, for the sale of liquors to be used as a beverage.

3. The absolute prohibition of the manufacture, importation, and sale of intoxicating liquors for such purpose - prohibition by the will of the people, expressed in due form of law, with the penalties deserved for a crime of such enormity.

4. The creation of a healthy public opinion upon the subject, by the active dissemination of truth in all the modes known to an enlightened philanthropy.

5. The election of good, honest men to administer the laws.

6. Persistence in effort to save individuals and communities from so direful a scourge against all forms of opposition and difficulty, till our success is complete and universal.

April 30, 1874

Milford Neck Lodge No. 69.I.O.G.T.

Meets every Monday evening in the Milford Neck M.E. Church. Visiting members are always welcome.

J.C. Clifton. L.D.

APPENDIX

CENSUS

TAX ASSESSMENTS

CEMETERIES

CENSUS

Early census taken was not very informative. They usually only had the name of the head of the household, number of males and number of females. Later they included ages and by 1850 the census takers were becoming a little more comprehensive. Here are some examples of later census records.

```
1850 Thompson, James      45        Farmer
              Sarah        43
              Anne E       16
              James A      12
              Daniel A     10
              Thomas       08
              Joshua H     05
              Mary E       5/12*

       Powell, Nancy       61

       Walker, James H     18


1860 Hill, Absolom        37        Farmer
              Rachel       29
              George       7
              Sarah E      4
              Sarah J      4/12*

       Quillen, William    13

       Quillen, Samuel     10

       Hutcheson, Edward   20        Comm School Teach
```

*Some of the census takers used fractions based on twelve months.

As you can see by the next one the census takers really became more informative by 1910.

```
1910 Thompson, Lydia A. Head F W 66 Wd Own Income
         Harvey A. Son M W 35 Md Farmer Farm Emp
         Sara V. Daug F W 33 S none
         Eliz R. Daug-in-law F W 28 Md none
```

Tax Assessments

The next few pages will show portions of tax assessments taken from early records.

1767 Squirrel Scalps:

Winlock Hall	12
Isaac Jester	10
Nathaniel Luff	60
George Manlove	20
James Thomlinson	12
John Thompson	08
Reynar Williams	25

1847	Real	Personal	Total
Isaac Jester	105	200	305
John R.T.Martin		200	200
John Martin	324	249	573
Lewis Passmore	120		120
Charles Polk	1700	234	1934
Margaret Thompson	168		168
James Thompson		342	342
John Thompson	890	405	1295
William Thompson	1160	468	1628

1849

	Real	Personal	Total
Isaac Jester	105	200	305
Nathan Livingston	120	216	336
John G. Martin(heirs)	390		390
Charles Polk	1700	216	1916
Capt. William Thompson	1160	450	1610
(add 168)James Thompson		543	543
(deduct 168)Marg.Thompson	168		168

1850

	Real	Personal	Total
Joshua Bennett	1330	383	1713
John Bennett	1331	482	1813
Absalom Hill	192		192

168

Issac Jester	105	235	340
Nathan Livingston	120	216	336
Charles Polk	1700	216	1916
William Thompson	183	324	507
Capt.William Thompson	1160	450	1610
John Thompson	890	430	1320
James Thompson	168	543	711

1852

Issac Jester

        163 acres, one story framed dwelling, kitchen, smokehouse, carriage house, stables, corn crib, all in common repair $340

1857

Charles Martin 1 sow, 7 pigs, $10 poll $150 $160

Absolom Hill 1 horse, 1 yoke oxen, 1 cow 2 yearlings,
        160 poll 150 $310

George Fowler 1 horse, 1 yoke oxen, 1 cow, 2 yearlings,
        110 poll 150 $260

1861

John Bennett	2014
Joshua Bennett	2418
Sarah E. & Susan E. Fowler	475
Ann R. Fowler	250
Absolom Hill	1183
Issac Jester	549
Mary D. Martin	42

1865

Absolom Hill 1 horse, 1 pr young oxen, 1 cow, 1 yearling
        poll   325

Issac R. Jester 1 pr oxen, 1 cow & calf, 4 head shoats
        poll   373

Mary D. Martin 2 head horses, 1 colt, 2 head cows, 1 yearling
        poll   150

James Thompson 2 head horses, 1 head cow, 6 head yearlings,

15 head sheep 7 head hogs   poll 629

Daniel A. Thompson   poll   200

1892

Issac Jester
      Farm 47 acres (30 acres available - 17 available - 17 Branch-woods) 2 story house, Barn & Stable, 1 horse, 1 cow, 1 yoke oxen 1270

Daniel A. Thompson   Farm 122 acres

      No.1   54 acres available, 68 acres woods, 1 1/2 story house 1080, fair outbuildings 680 (tenant - Nathaniel French)

      No. 2 Farm 16 acres, store, Two Story house, stable (tenant self) 1500

      No. 3 Farm 34 acres Two story house, stable 14 acres   available 280   15 wood 180, 5 cripple 25, 21 marsh 21

      No. 4 Steam Saw Mill 500, 3 horses 150, 6 cows 90, 4 steers   50,   Poll
300   Total 4856

TOMBSTONES OF ABSALOM HILL & RACHEL D. HILL
Which are in Odd Fellows Cemetery, Milford
Taken by Roland Beebe

The Bennett Cemetery, as listed in the Tatnall Tombstone Collection, is located North of the Sardis Methodist Church on the right way back in the field.

*Thompson Joshua,son James & Sarah b Apr 11,1845 d Apr 3, 1879

*Age 33 Mary, wife of Daniel d Dec 12, 1869
*   Mary E., her daughter d Dec 1, 1869

*Age 65 James d Jul 17, 1869
*   Thomas, son James & Sarah b May 2, 1842
                    d Sep 13, 1866
*Sarah Powell, wife of James b Sep 25 1804
                    d Feb 1, 1866

French, Lewis, son of Samuel & Annie d July 9, 1891

*Jester, Joseph, son Geo. H & Sarah E. b Apr 9, 1881 d Jul 30, 1882

Parsons, Penelope, wife of Joseph d May 7, 1970

*Peet, Eliza b sept 8, 1787 d Mar 10, 1870

My wife and I went back to this site and found that some of the tombstones are still there. I have marked these, in the above list, with an asterisk. On the next three pages you will find the inscriptions from those remaining stones.

MARY E
Daughter of Daniel and
Mary EM Thompson
12-1-1869 Born
7-17-1870 Died
****

In Memory of

James S. Thompson
Departed this life
July 17, 1869
Aged about 65 years
****

In memory of

Sarah Powell
wife of
James Thompson
Born SEP 25 1804
Departed this life
FEB 1 1866
Aged 61 yrs 4 mos 6 days
****

Mary E.M.
wife of
Daniel A. Thompson
Died 12-12-1869
Aged 33 yrs 5 mos 2 days

Husband and child, I must leave you
Leave - Yes, leave you all alone:
But my blessed Saviour calls me
Calls me to a heav-enly home.

Farewell sweet sister, thou shalt ever be
A star to guide me up to heaven and thee
****

In memory of

Thomas A.
son of
James & Sarah
Thompson
Born May 2 1843
Departed this life
Sep 13 1866
Aged 24 yrs 4 mos
11 days
****

In memory of

Joshua H Thompson
Son of James &
Sarah Thompson

Born April 11 1845
Died April 3 1879
Aged 33 yrs 11 mos
& 22 days
****

Joseph H

Son of George H &
Sarah E Jester
Born
April 7 1881
Died
July 30 1882
Gone but not forgotten
****

In memory of

Eliza Peet
Born Sep 4 1797
Died June 10 1870
Aged 72 yrs 6 mos & 2 days
****

BIBLIOGRAPHY

Much of the early history for this work was obtained from reading former historians. Since this is not a text book, I have made no attempt to cite volume or page.

Winfred Grogory, American newspapers 1821 - 1936 (1937 - Kraus Reprint Corp., New York 1967)

George B. Hynson, Historical Etchings of Milford & Vicinity (1899)

J. Thomas Scharf, History of Delaware (1888 - L.J. Richards & Company)

J.M. Runk, Biographical and Genealogical History of Delaware (1899)

Henry Clay Conrad, A History of the State of Delaware (published by author at Wilmington, Delaware 1908)

William M. Lytle Forrest R. Holdcamper, Merchant Steam Vessels of the United States (17900 - 1868)

Other historical references:

Mildred Coverdale, Frederica Trinity United Methodist Church and Two Charges (1978)

E. Dallas Hitchens & E. Millis Hurley, Milford, Delaware & The Milford Area after 1776 (Delaware Genealogical Society 1985)

Harold B. Hancock with M. Catherine Downing, Businesses and Industries of Milford, Delaware 1787 - 1987 (Milford Historical Society 1987)

E. Dallas Hitchens, The Milford, Delaware Area Before 1776 (Shawnee Printing 1976)

Material derived from the Delaware State Archives, Dover, Delaware (used by permission):

Photographs:

> 8/660 Kirby's School
> 8/558 Bennett's Gate School
> 8/726 Pine Grove School
> 8/528a John Wesley Colored School
> 8/528c John Wesley Colored School, 1921

Information from:

Tax Assessment Records 1700's & 1800's
Census Records 1800's & 1900's

Other State Offices Visited:

Kent County Recorder of Deeds
Kent County Recorder of Wills
Sussex County Recorder of Deeds
Sussex County Recorder of Wills

Libraries & Museums visited:

Milford Library, Milford, Delaware
Delaware State Library, Dover, Delaware
Barratt's Chapel & Museum, Frederica, Delaware

Newspapers used: Milford Chronicle, Delaware State News, Smyrna Times, State Sentinel, Peninsular News & Advertiser, The Rescue, Sussex News

Personal Interviews:

Mr. J. Spencer Willis
Mr. Burton D. Willis
James & Theresa Webb
Albert & Sarah Webb
Mr. & Mrs. Purnell Powell
Walter & Lillian Wilkerson